DARTMOOR PRISON

A COMPLETE ILLUSTRATED HISTORY

VOLUME ONE – THE WAR PRISON 1809-1816

'Parcere Subjectis'

Ron Joy

HALSGROVE

First published in Great Britain in 2002

British Library Cataloguing-in-Publication Data
A CIP record for this title is available from the British Library

ISBN 1 84114 200 X

HALSGROVE

Halsgrove House
Lower Moor Way
Tiverton, Devon EX16 6SS
Tel: 01884 243242
Fax: 01884 243325
email: sales@halsgrove.com
website: www.halsgrove.com

Printed and bound in Great Britain by Bookcraft (Bath) Ltd, Midsomer Norton

FOREWORD

The forbidding grey granite walls of Dartmoor Prison have dominated the Devon skyline for nearly two hundred years, and its name and reputation have resonated around the world. The grim façade is famous, and belies the nature of the life within. Its full history has never before been told in such a sweeping way.

Ron Joy has worked at Dartmoor for half his lifetime, and has researched his subject with passion in the UK and USA. The resulting book is a mixture of recorded history, anecdote and one man's impressions and recollections.

Set down in two volumes, he takes us from the earliest years as a prisoner-of-war camp to its use as a medium high-security facility for convicted offenders in 1990. Richly illustrated with pictures, he has produced a history which lives, and tales which will amuse and sometimes shock you. As you read, you will be marching with the first draft of prisoners of war from Plymouth to the new facility, and living amongst them in the Blocks. You will marvel at the persistence of man, and the desire to survive which exists in most prisoners, whatever the circumstances.

I was Deputy Governor from 1990, and Governor from 1994–2001. I was proud to serve with fine men and women, who epitomised all that was best in human nature, showing total commitment to a difficult and often dangerous task. Together, we changed Dartmoor to a modern regime, tautly managed and delivering security for the community and rehabilitation for the offender. The staff are often unsung and unappreciated by those pursuing their own agendas, and in reading this book I hope that you will be able to gain some understanding of the immense difficulties of working in such an environment, and the pressures.

It is, finally, a tale of human endeavour of those so detained and those detaining them, often against the odds. The human spirit survives even in such difficult and restrictive conditions, and humour is everywhere.

These volumes have pride of place on my bookshelves, so they will on yours.

John Lawrence
Governor, Dartmoor Prison, 1994–2001
Tavistock, Devon, June 2002

*View of Dartmoor Prison from above the
old dairy, pre-1932 mutiny.*

Virgil's Aeneid

Tu regere imperio populos, Romane, memento.
(Hae tibi erunt artes) pacique imponere morem,
Parcere subjectis* et debellare superbos.

translation:
You, Roman, make your task to rule nations by your Government.
(These shall be your skills)[1] to impose ordered ways
upon a state of peace, to spare those who have submitted and to
subdue the arrogant.

Author: Principal Officer, Ron Joy.

*Generally held to mean 'spare or pity the vanquished' i.e. those who have already submitted (those who have been captured).
[1]Or '(Be these your arts)' i.e. to impose the rule of peace, to spare the conquered and abase the proud.

Rundlestone area – the cottage top left was
the home of Prison Stoker Bernard Hext.

CONTENTS

ACKNOWLEDGEMENTS

Many thanks to the following for their invaluable word-of-mouth recollections and access to private documents: Officer Dave Bone, last man to ride mounted patrol (pony patrol) at Dartmoor Prison; John Dymond, Australia, for information on William Dymond, warder Dartmoor Convict Prison 1873, later governor of an Australian prison; Officer C. Elcombe, last man to fire a rifle at Dartmoor Prison; Chilli Frampton, former officer circa 1932, later farm manager; Richard Elmer Johnson, information on Francis Dolphin, ex-1812 war prisoner; Chief Officer 1 Lenaghan, Dartmoor Prison; Marjorie Mace (Putt), information on Capt Stacey, ex-1812 war prisoner; Stan Mutton, officer circa 1932; Mr Tiley, ex-steward Dartmoor Prison (joined 1904); Officer Pinney, circa 1932 Dartmoor Prison; Joan and Stan Von Sternberg, USA information on Fort Sewell; Cyril Penny, officer circa 1932; Chief Officer 1 Dennis Sutton re German prisoners; Reg Gauci re transported convicts.

The prison leat in the foreground, with war prisons Nos 4, 5, 6 and 7 in the background.

INTRODUCTION

In 1968 I was a basic grade prison officer (discipline) just posted to HMP Dartmoor from Exeter Prison. I had just completed my induction course at Dartmoor under very experienced prison officers and felt a sense of complete bewilderment as I walked towards the entrance gate from inside the prison. My target was the duty boards between the gates where I would find out what duty would await me at 7am the next day.

I saw that I would be on Farm 1 party, working, naturally, with experienced officers who would train me. The following day I carried out my usual duties inside the prison and then collected Farm 1 party from the tally point. We made our way to the farm, myself and 15 convicts. We call the convicts inmates now but back then they were known strictly as the convicts.

A meeting with the farm manager, Chilli Frampton, and all discipline officers on the farm parties always took place first to establish what work was to be done that day. The farm manager said to me first, 'Take four convicts and go down to the French and American cemeteries and give them a tidy up, we are expecting some American visitors soon.' French and American cemeteries? Though I had heard of them, I was puzzled about the American cemetery. As I was collecting the necessary tools for my new party from the farm tool store, I said to my fellow officer, 'Why is it the American cemetery?' He turned to me with a snarl and said, 'Never mind why, get moving and get a grip of the four convicts or the chief officer will get a grip of you.'

Taking my party and lining them up into two-by-twos, I marched them down there and found, to my surprise, that there were two separate cemeteries, each with its own granite memorial. I set the convicts to work on clearing them and vowed that I would enlighten myself, and perhaps others. So I commenced my studies. This took me to the prison archives, the Duchy of Cornwall offices in London, the Home Office archives, also in London, the Public Record Office, even Bideford Art Gallery; and many other places which would throw some light on the history of Dartmoor Prison.

My talks with several former prison officers who were working between 1927 and 1939, around the years of the 1932 mutiny, gave me a wealth of information on those difficult years. Of course these men, who were serving at the time of the mutiny, served under officers who were working at the turn of the century. They had many valuable stories and information. Friends in the United States, particularly those in New York and Massachusetts, were an enormous help with filling in the American connection.

Dartmoor Prison is unique in having a town built around it for the sole purpose of the prison. With the exception of the Plume of Feathers pub and several cottages up Plymouth Hill, the prison was the first building in what would later become Princetown. Over a period of one-hundred-and-fifty years, convicts made all the roads in the town and kept them in good order when they were finished. They built the walls on the prison estates and in the village, as well as the officers' houses and a prison officers' school. The convicts worked on the extensive estates, clearing stone and draining the bogs, doing forestry and farming, while the hard-labour party worked the prison quarry. The incredible granite prison buildings were built by the convicts with superb skill.

Above: *The oldest structure on prison land, Fice's Well, with the date 1568 on lintel.*
Right: *The wall built by convicts to protect Fice's Well from damage by cattle.*

Chapter One
TYRWHITT'S DREAM

Why do the bleak buildings of Dartmoor Prison stand where they do, so forlorn amongst the magical granite tors? Their construction had nothing to do with convicts and punishments or anything of that ilk. This forbidding place initially was built to house innocent men; innocent in that their only crime was to fight for their country; prisoners of war, both French, American and of other nations.

During my service part of my duties was to act as the prison historian which often involved showing some French and many American visitors around Dartmoor Prison. I was able to show them the places where their forebears were held during the Napoleonic Wars and the war of 1812, places which were, and still are, largely unknown by visitors and staff.

Its story starts around the year 1771 when George III was on the throne and the feelings of the French were running high against the English. At this time there were no roads and little habitation on this part of the moor; the land was empty but for the tenements – the name given to the ancient farms of the area – and the scars of activities such as tin mining. On 17 July 1771 an advertisement appeared in a Westcountry publication inviting interested parties to attend a meeting at Moretonhampstead to consider a scheme for constructing a road across Dartmoor from the town to Tavistock. It went well and events proceeded quickly following it.

In 1772 an Act was passed for construction of the road and authority obtained for the work to proceed. It was this turnpike road, which when completed, was the catalyst for the building of Dartmoor Prison. Without it the prison and the village of Princetown might never have existed. Access to the moor was now relatively easy and several people, including those called 'improvers' by many, moved in. One of the earliest improvers was a Mr Gullett who began farming at Princehall in about 1780 on one of the ancient tenements.

Until the coming of the turnpike road, packhorses were the only means of transport to convey goods and people across the desolate moors. They had to cross rivers and streams using the ancient clapper bridges which stood at such places as Postbridge, Dartmeet, Ockery and Beardown. Clapper bridges were built by placing large slabs of granite across the often swiftly-flowing water, though the difficulties of lifting and moving such a heavy material without the benefit of modern machinery and lifting gear, necessarily limited the size of the slabs that could be used. Where the river was too wide for one slab, a single clapper and then central pillars were built in order to achieve the desired span.

The old packhorse trails precluded wheeled traffic but as soon as the turnpike road was complete, it arrived, bringing a new population to the area. At the centre of all this activity was Thomas Tyrwhitt. Born in Wickham Bishops, near London, on 12 August 1762, he was a son of the rector of that parish, educated at Eton and Christchurch, Oxford. He took an MA Degree in 1787, aged twenty-five. The Dean of Christchurch introduced him to the Prince of Wales,

Sketch of a clapper bridge on the prison estates, too wide for one clapper, showing how it was constructed.

A typical clapper bridge on prison estates, allowing movement of convicts and staff.

later to be George IV, and a friendship grew between Thomas, the common man aged eighteen years, and the Prince of Wales, heir to the throne.

In 1786, when only twenty-four, Thomas was appointed as auditor to the Duchy of Cornwall. On the death of Lord Dartmouth, Lord Warden of the Stannaries, Tyrwhitt succeeded him in that impressive post and later was appointed Vice Admiral of the Counties of Devon and Cornwall. He was also Colonel of the First Cornish Militia, the tough Cornish miners. Tyrwhitt represented Okehampton in Parliament from 1796–1802 and Plymouth from 1806–12, when he was appointed Gentleman Usher of the Black Rod, a post he held for twenty years.

Thomas Tyrwhitt died on 24 February 1833 at Calais in France while returning from a holiday there. He was described as being a small, active man who remained a bachelor. According to Governor Thompson's book,[1] his manners were pleasant and he was courteous. As the memorial tablet in Princetown Church reads:

> *His name and memory are inseparable from all the great works on Dartmoor and cannot cease to be honoured in this district.*

Here we have a man who had strong links with the Prince of Wales, the owner of much of Dartmoor, strong ties with the Government as a Member of Parliament, and high office with the Admiralty as Vice Admiral of Devon and Cornwall. He was also MP for Plymouth, with links to its naval dockyards. In 1785 he was granted a lease on Dartmoor which was renewed on 15 September 1812. At 2285 acres, two roods and 34 perches, it was a sizeable estate.

Thomas Tyrwhitt's dream to open up the moor for his employer, the Prince of Wales, seemed to be gathering momentum. In 1785 he built an inn which he named the Plume of Feathers after the heraldic symbol of the Prince of Wales. The inn was accompanied by some cottages on what is now called Plymouth Hill to house the people who worked on Tyrwhitt's estate. The oldest lease for the Plume of Feathers (circa 1785) seen by the author is dated 20 April 1808,

[1] Basil Thompson was governor at Darmoor Prison for seven years in the late-nineteenth century. His book *The Story of Dartmoor Prison* (Heineman 1907) has been a source of much information by the present author.

Above left: *The Plume of Feathers Inn, built 1785, the oldest building in Princetown, as it was in 1920, and* (above) *as it looks in more recent times.* Left: *A view entering Princetown, early-nineteenth century.*

twenty-three years after the inn was built and before the prison was completed in 1809. The lease was to one Robert Lane, victualler. The acreage of the Plume at that time was 31 acres, three roods and three perches. The lease for the first twenty-three years of the Plume's life appears to be missing but may yet come to light.

Thomas Tyrwhitt was determined to change the high barren wastelands of the moor which had been unpopulated since the departure of the old tin miners; land which was approaching 1500 feet above sea level, exposed on all sides to the biting wind, and where the acidity of the soil, lack of shelter, thick mists and very low temperatures made the growing of crops almost impossible.

A view of a building at Ockery, known as Trena Bridge on prison maps.

Having spent from 1968–92 as a prison officer at Dartmoor, and having also visited the prison every day from then until the year 2000, the author can vouch for the cruel winter weather and high rainfall. Most of us lived in official quarters with small gardens, and trying to grow flowers was a thankless task.

But Tyrwhitt held steadfastly to his plan to open up the vast wastelands in the hope that by building a model town – to be named Prince's Town after his friend and employer – he might bring commercial interest to the area, accruing profits for the Duchy and the Prince of Wales, and royal favour for himself. At Ockery Bridge, named as Trena Bridge on prison maps, Tyrwhitt built structures listed as Miller's House and a mill alongside the Blackabrook river.

The Miller's House and the Plume of Feathers seem to owe their appearance to buildings that Tyrwhitt had seen on his travels to Russia. The No. 7 barrack block in the barracks compound was built later but also reflects the style of the Plume in exterior appearance.

It seems likely that Tyrwhitt also designed the Tor Royal house, including the lodges and farm buildings. Moor stone for the buildings was plentiful, but wood, unobtainable on Dartmoor, was brought from Plymouth. Tor Royal followed the usual Westcountry style of building which was low and squat to be out of the wind. As a very old Princetown resident once told me:

Like its people, Princetown buildings are short, thick set and hard, you mustn't grow taller than the hedges or stone walls or you will get your head blowed off and you will get your body covered in 'ammil' [ice].

It is a good description from Cliff Waycott, a ninety-year-old grandson of an old Dartmoor warder.

Much of Tyrwhitt's time was spent at Tor Royal and, after several unsuccessful attempts, he finally succeeded in growing a crop of flax on one of the less exposed sites of his estates, and probably during a period of favourable weather. It gained him a medal from the Bath Agricultural Society. Following this success the next requirement was improvement to the access roads on the moor that would make Tyrwhitt's model town possible.

But things were to take something of a different turn when in 1803 peace was once again shattered and war was declared between England and France.

Tor Royal, home of Thomas Tyrwhitt, c.1785.

THE HULKS

Men taken prisoner in the subsequent actions were brought to England to be placed in prisoner-of-war depots, primarily the hulks moored on the south coast at Plymouth, Chatham and Portsmouth, amongst others. The French kept in the hulks at Plymouth were extremely troublesome and a constant source of worry to the Transport Board, posing as they did, a threat to the nearby naval dockyards and arsenals.

The following information, along with letters held by Plymouth and West Devon Record Office, written by Captain Hawkins RN, superintendent of prisons in Plymouth, helps to give an insight into the times and conditions prevailing in the prison hulks at dock. Some 2000 French and American prisoners of war were held in the old Mill Prison (rebuilt in 1799 and then known as Millbay Prison) in the years 1812–15.

The *Le Brave* was a hulk which was the former French ship *Formidable* of 80 guns. It was captured on 3 November 1805 by Sir Richard John Strachan's squadron after escaping from Trafalgar. *Le Brave* became the HQ ship of Captain Edward Hawkins, superintendent of prisons and prison ships. He became agent for prisoners of war at Plymouth after the death of Captain Osiah Rogers RN on 2 May at Mill Prison.

The Transport Board then appointed Captain Edward Pellowe as agent for prisoners of war at Mill Prison, allowing Captain Hawkins to revert to his post as superintendent of ships afloat at Plymouth. Up to 800 prisoners were held on board *Le Brave.*

El Firm was the former Spanish 74-gun vessel captured by Sir Robert Calder in July 1805 off Ferrol. It was first commissioned as a prison ship at Plymouth on 23 February 1808 and subsequently held up to 750 prisoners.

San Ysidro and *San Nicolas* were both Spanish 80-gun ships captured by Sir John Jervis KB off Cape St Vincent in February 1797. Both were in use as prison ships by October 1805 and each was to hold up to 750 prisoners of war.

Hector was a French 74-gun vessel captured by Lord Rodney in his victory of 12 April 1782 and became a prison ship by December 1807, holding up to 700 men. The first Americans to arrive at Dartmoor in 1813 came from the *Hector.*

Le Caton was also a French 74-gun ship captured by Lord Hood in the Mona Passage on 1 April 1782. It became a prison ship by October 1805 and was the hospital ship which lay off Saltash in 1811.

Genereux was a French 64-gun ship captured by Rear Admiral Lord Nelson in the Mediterranean on 18 February 1800, having escaped from Nelson's victory in Aboukir Bay in August 1798. A prison ship by October 1805, it held up to 750 prisoners.

L'oiseau was the former French frigate *Cleopatre* of 36 guns and was captured on 18 June 1793 off the Start. *The Nymph* had 36 guns and became a prison ship by February 1807, holding 300 men.

Bienfaisant was a French 64-gun vessel captured in 1758. It had become a prison ship by June 1797 and was a prison convalescent ship in 1802.

Europe was an old British ship with 64 guns built in 1766. It formed part of the North American Squadron from 1779–80. It became a prison ship holding 700 men by June 1797 and was taken out of service in December 1811 but returned to use because of severe overcrowding in other hulks in September 1813.

Ganges and *Vanguard* became prison ships by 18 December 1811 and held up to 750 men each. The *Prince* acted as a prison ship off Plymouth between 24 January and 11 April 1808, and again was brought back into service because of overcrowding.

The *San Pareil* was a Spanish ship of 80 guns captured off Ferrol on 22 July 1805. It was a prison ship by May 1809. These hulks afforded substantial accommodation for prioners of war along the south coast. There were also many other hulks and prisons at this time, as far afield as Scotland, Liverpool and Kergilliack (between Penryn and Falmouth). Prisoners were removed around the end of 1797 from Kergilliack because they were too far from the superintendent of the Transport Board. At Kergilliack it was stated that the treatment of prisoners had been neglected and alleged that bread had been made with

A painting of the hulks at Plymouth, depicted by a convict historian.

bad corn mixed with chaff. Following an investigation into these allegations it was reported that although the bread was of inferior quality there was no evidence of chaff being mixed with the corn.

Here follow some letters written to, and by, Captain Hawkins, taken from his papers:

Letter written to Captain Hawkins in 1810:

In reply to your letter of this date I acquaint you that you may move as many of the prisoners from the Prince *to the* Brave *tomorrow as you can, and that launches shall be sent to remove the remainder on Monday morning. I am Sir, your most obedient servant, A Young.*

Letter regarding payment of accounts to the Transport Board from Captain Hawkins:

Paid the prisoners employed on board the Le Caton *hospital ship the sum of £21.2s.4d.*

There is no mention of how many prisoners were employed or what the period of time was. It shows that there were prisoner-employees who received wages for their work as servants. The honesty in those distant days is sometimes remarkable. Even a man who had deserted his English ship for an American one would, on being captured, be paid the prize money owing from his service on the previous English ship:

Paid 743 prisoners three pence per man, also paid eight Danes at Mill Prison £1.0s.4d.

Again there is no period of time mentioned. The date stamp on the letters records, 'Paid, 1 Sept. 1810'.

The letter below was sent to Captain Hawkins instructing him to pay the Danish prisoners. The following instruction was one which agents were required to sign:

Agents for the prisoners of war at _____ doth voluntarily make oath that every article of disbursement inserted in the foregoing account amounting to £_____ is just and true, and that the money was really and truly paid to the persons, and for the services and things thereon respectfully mentioned, and to and for no other whatsoever.
Sworn before me at _____. This day of _____
Agent _____

Letter from Captain Hawkins dated 1 September 1813:

Sir,
A number of prisoners having been sent from Dartmoor to the prison ships,
upwards of 200 of them have the Itch and a number very bad indeed. The surgeon
of the Hector, *where they are having apartments, is out of Itch ointment and that*
he has applied to the Transport Board for a supply. But no order has arrived to
supply him, and to request you will place an order on temporary supply of
ointment for the said prisoners.

Edward Hawkins.

Letter dated 10 October 1813:

Sir,
I beg to inform you the prison ships are filling fast, and many sick and wounded
are coming from Spain I beg to submit to your considering the moving of some to
Dartmoor if there is room. For if any considerable number arrive from Spain we
should be quite filled up, and Admiral Sir M. Calder is always desirous for having
room for three or four hundred at a moment's notice.

E.H.

These letters, and there are many in Hawkins' papers, show the vast numbers
of prisoners moved to and from Dartmoor Depot (as it was then known) at this
time. The list below shows the staff on board a hulk. There were navy
personnel and army/navy personnel as follows:

Naval Personnel
1	*lieutenant RN in charge*
1	*surgeon*
1	*gunner*
1	*boatswain*
1	*carpenter*
1	*cook*
1	*purser*
1	*master's mate*
2	*midshipmen*
1	*purser's steward*
15	*seamen*
2	*boys 2nd class*
3	*boys 3rd class*
31	*total on hulk*

Army on each hulk
1	*lieutenant in charge*
1	*ensign*
1	*corporal*
35	*militia soldiers*
38	*total*

This made a total of 69 altogether on a hulk. Bearing in mind that many hulks
held 750 prisoners, this was a necessary number of staff members.

Parole agents at the time included:

Joseph Grubble	*Ashburton*	*Devon*
Mr Todd	*Andover*	*Hants*
John Wood	*Ashburn* [sic]	*Derbys*
Joseph Farnell	*Ashby-de-la-Zouch*	*Leics*
John Dun	*Alvesford* [sic]	*Hants*
Walter Churchy	*Brecon*	*Wales*
John Penny	*Bishops Waltham*	*Hants*
Thomas Welsford	*Crediton*	*Devon*

J. Bower	Chesterfield	Derbys
Stephen Spittigue	Launceston	Cornwall
Samuel Ebrall	Lichfield	Leics
Edward Powys	Leck	Leics
Frances Allen	Montgomery	Wales
John Ponsford	Moretonhampstead	Devon
A.P. Tozer	Okehampton	Devon
James Cairnes	Peebles	
Thomas Inchmarch	Tiverton	Devon
Christopher Smith	Thame	
George Messiter	Wincanton	Somerset
John Stevenson	Northampton	Northampton
Herbert Lewes	Reading	Berks
John Crapper	Wantage	Oxon

The list of parole officers based all over Britain illustrates just how many prisoners were allowed out on parole to all the different parole towns.

ROCKY ROAD TO A WAR PRISON

In October 1808, seven months before the Dartmoor Depot received its first prisoners from the hulks, Captain Isaac Cotsgrave RN, agent for prisons at Plymouth, was appointed agent for Dartmoor at his own request. George McGrath, the surgeon at Mill Prison, was recommended for the same post at Dartmoor but instead the Admiralty chose Mr William Dykar who had served in the American War of Independence 1775. This was a mistake as he seemed to be a typical naval surgeon of that time. He was ignorant, not overly skilful and, as proved later by the Americans, an unsympathetic man to all, especially those whom he disliked.

An extract from the *Bristol Mirror* 13 July 1805 reads:

The Prince of Wales is about to erect at his own expense a chapel at Prince's Town, in the Forest of Dartmoor under the direction of Thomas Tyrwhitt Esq. Lord Warden of the Stannaries. Mr Thomas Tyrwhitt has suggested to the Government the propriety of erecting, near the above, a building for the deposit of such prisoners of war, who can, without difficulty be conveyed up the River Tamar and landed within a few miles of the spot. It is said that this plan be acted upon forthwith and also for the barracks to be erected for a proportionate number of troops. As mentioned the Admiralty has a section called the Transport Board who are responsible for 'the care of sick and wounded seamen and prisoners of war.'

After the inspection near Thomas Tyrwhitt's lodges the Transport Board wrote a letter to their superiors thus:

Land near Thomas Tyrwhitt's lodges would make an admirable area for a prison to house there prisoners of war and remove them away from the dockyards and arsenals, we have already approached a certain Thomas Tyrwhitt who has given his consent, on behalf of the Prince of Wales, to the Transport Board having whatever quantity of the moor they may wish to take for a prison without charge to the public under an Act of Parliament to transfer the land from the Duchy of Cornwall to the Crown.

The Act was never passed but a lease of 390 acres leasehold for ninety-nine years was drawn up in the first instance. Ground rent for the lease of 390 acres, one rood, 34 perches for ninety-nine years was as follows:

First thirty years	£41.7s.6d.
Second thirty years	£61.0s.0d.
Remaining thirty-nine years	£91.5s.0d.
Tota	£193.12s.6d.

As Thomas Tyrwhitt's heart was set on this, laws were quickly passed to allow the prison to go ahead. The Transport Board introduced Tyrwhitt to an architect by the name of Daniel Asher Alexander. When Alexander visited Tor Royal for the first time on 17 July 1805 he was then at the height of an established reputation. The London Docks, with his three groups of warehouses, had been opened only six months earlier and other work for well-known and influential clients was in progress. Alexander had some power and, more importantly, some valuable contacts in the capital.

Together Alexander and Tyrwhitt examined a variety of locations on Dartmoor and finally decided on a place near Tyrwhitt's lodges, on North Hessary Tor slopes. Bearing in mind the previous correspondence this was a foregone conclusion. Thomas Tyrwhitt had already selected the site because it would create the settlement which he had always wanted. It was, however, totally inappropriate for the housing of prisoners. To get to the proposed prison the men would have to be marched across approximately 18 miles of some of the roughest country in England from the hulks and prisons at Dock. It was not possible to get a ship of any kind up the Tamar.

The weather up on Dartmoor was awful and the death toll in the first few years of opening was very high and would lead to serious discussions and proposals in Parliament for the abandonment of the prison. Even on the moor itself there were far better places, perhaps at a lower elevation and nearer the roads to Plymouth. The only reason for choosing the site was its proximity to the newly constructed turnpike road from Moretonhampstead to Ashburton. This was frequented by carriers who would be content to sell their wares at the future Prince's Town, which would be easier than transporting them all the way to Plymouth.

And, of course, Tyrwhitt was determined to make his great dreams come to fruition. After he had discussed it with Alexander, the architect left for his office in London to draw up plans for the building of a war prison.

Eventually the plans were completed but his first estimate of £86 423.13s.4d. frightened the Admiralty who ordered a reduction in size and number of buildings. Alexander complied with the instructions and prepared a second set of drawings. He cut down the area inside the boundary wall from 23 acres to 15 acres, two roods. The reduced estimated cost was £70 146.4s.10d.

An early depiction of the five original war prisons, 1809, before two more were added. The original caption read: 'Prospective View of the War-Prison near Tor-Royal upon Dartmoor, designed for the accommodation of 10,000 Men with Barracks for 2,000 men at short distance but not represented in the Plan. D. Alexander, Architect.'

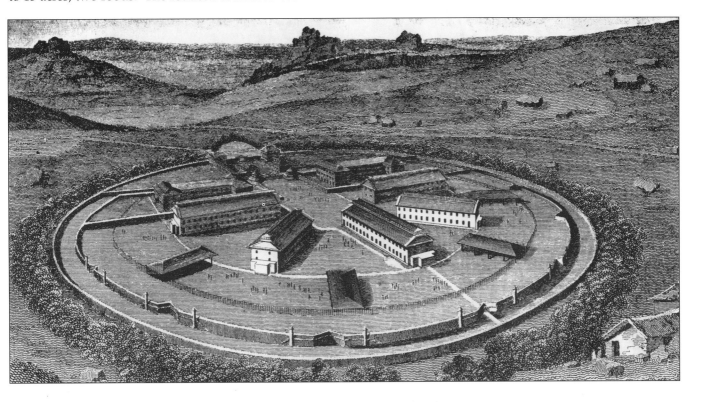

There were five war prisons, each to house 1000 men on two levels. There would be a third level, called the cockloft, to allow for exercise during wet weather. The cockloft would also later be used for holding prisoners, as more than 1500 men were held in each war prison for most of the time. An infirmary prison was needed to cater for a large prisoner population, with quarters for staff, surgeons and others. A petty officers' prison was to be completely separate from the five war prisons, as well as staff houses for the agent, the deputy, the surgeons and others.

There were barracks for at least 1000 troops. In total 11 barrack blocks were built, ranging from very large three-storey buildings to a single house for the barrack sergeant. A water supply was taken from Spriddle Lake, a feeder of the River Walkham about four miles from the prison. Water was to be transported in open leats to all areas of the war prisons. The freshwater leat would enter the building, pass under the latrines and exit as foul water.

The military officers' mess would later become the prison officers' mess and is now the High Moorland Visitors' Centre.

Tenders were sent from Plymouth. The highest seen by the author was for £115 337.0s.0d., from Messrs Ravell & Co. The second was from a builder called Sheppard & Co. who costed the plans to be £84 828.0s.0d., and the third, winning tender was submitted by a firm called Isbell, Rowe & Co. at £66 815.0s.0d. – the price of a small modern bungalow. Isbell, Rowe's price was below the estimate made by Alexander and was accepted by the Admiralty. There was a lot of additional expense, normal for contract works, and the total cost was approximately £75 000.

It seems that during the construction of the war prisons, the only way Isbell, Rowe could break even was by skimping on the buildings. The buildings were moor stone with slate roofs and were actually quite permanent. Granite was chosen because it was the cheapest material to be had, being obtainable for the cost of collection and quarrying alone. Bricks were unobtainable anywhere near the proposed site and transportation costs from Plymouth, along rough moorland roads, would have been enormous. The granite blocks, which were huge, were advantageous for security as well.

The collection of moor stone began on the open moor near the prison but could not satisfy the vast quantities required. A quarry was opened and named Herne Hole and is the present prison quarry. Then a tramway was laid to convey the granite from the quarry to the prison site.

As a former building contractor, an item in the contract seems astounding to the author. It stipulated that 'the Admiralty can terminate the contract at any moment on the proclamation of peace'. Just where this would leave the contractor is open to argument but it seems certain that he would have been greatly out of pocket, owing to materials purchased, wages paid and no payment from the Admiralty. It placed the contractor in a precarious position.

The line of the tramway to Herne Hole is still visible and is the track used by the present convicts from the back gate of the prison to the quarry. The route passes between Pig Field and Rocky Field, through Cemetery Field and under the main road through a tunnel.

In 1806 the contract commenced and, as the contractor had submitted a low price, speed was of the essence. The more quickly the prison was built, the lower the labour costs and the greater the profit. The so-called foundation stone was laid officially on 20 March 1806 by Sir Thomas Tyrwhitt; 'so-called' because in twenty years the author never saw or heard of a foundation stone at the prison. It is doubtful that there ever was one. Perhaps a foundation stone was laid to commemorate the commencement of the contract to build five prisons.

Three drawings of the building of the war prisons by Samuel Prout 'Dartmoor Prison during construction, June 1807'. The photograph (below), shows an existing part of the petty officers' prison, as depicted on the right-hand side of bottom drawing.

Right: *Author's sketch of war prison No. 2 from an original plan.*
Below: *Names of fields on the prison estates.*

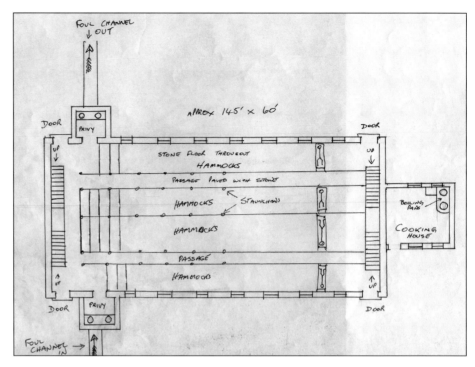

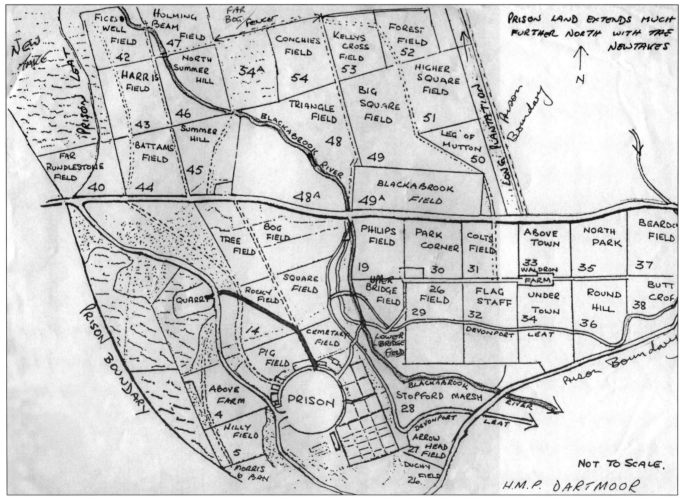

The contractor hired Cornish masons, renowned for hard work, to get the work underway speedily. The labour had to be cheap as it was expected that labour costs would make up 75 per cent of the contract price. It was at first proposed to bring masons down from the Yorkshire moors but Alexander warned that 'the masons in the country are beginning to rouse'. The Cornish could be hired from a shorter distance for lower wages and without the threat of rebellion for better wages and conditions.

There was a lot of water on the site, which Alexander proposed could be used to wash away the surface peat to lower parts of the moor without having to carry out excavations. This was real optimism on his part as the peat is more than six feet thick in places. Work did proceed quickly, however, though apparently without the necessary supervision to ensure the contractor carried out the correct specifications. It seems today that the boundary wall has been re-built in many places. Commenting as a former stonemason, experienced in building granite walls, the early construction methods left many problems to be dealt with during the author's term of office.

This picture of the rebuilding of part of boundary wall in the 1970s shows how poorly this wall was built some time between 1806 and 1809.

The wall was built without much bonding or 'tying in' and was made from relatively small granite stones, resembling what I would call in my days as a stonemason, 'a bag of mussels'. It was liable to collapse at any time and at only eight feet high was not a security barrier: this was the job of armed sentries on the inner battlements. The wall was later built to 12 feet in height.

Meanwhile, the Cornish masons had also 'started to rouse', and the cost of their labour had risen by 20 per cent. Timber was scarce owing to the blockade of Prussian ports. When the contract commenced timber was priced at £5 per load which soon jumped to £7, then in December 1806 to £8, with prices still rising. The contractor first tried to make the Admiralty pay for the increased costs of timber to avoid bankruptcy. He then stated that in order to save his family from ruin he would immediately sack all of the workmen and walk away, leaving the buildings to their fate. This finally alerted the Admiralty to the situation, with the urgency of moving prisoners away from the docks and arsenals still pressing. The threat from the contractor was real. Perhaps there was also some pressure from behind the scenes from Tyrwhitt, as the Admiralty soon agreed to supply the necessary timber at valuation. A large quantity of ships was being built and repaired at this time so a supply of timber was kept at the docks, some of it new, with a great deal from broken-up ships belonging to the Royal Navy.

British Naval Forces inventories at the Devon Record Office show the amount of timber that would have been available. Included below is the list from 1 January 1813:

Ships at Sea
79 ships of the line
9 ships 50–44 guns
122 frigates
77 sloops
161 brigs
4 bombs [?]
54 cutters
52 schooners

In port being fitted out
34 ships of the line
11 ships 50–44 guns
29 frigates
Several hospital ships
Several prison ships

Ordinary and Repairing
77 ships of the line
10 ships 50–44 guns
70 frigates
37 sloops
3 bombs [?]
11 brigs
1 cutter
2 schooners

In building
29 ships of the line
4 ships 50–44 guns
15 frigates
5 sloops
3 brigs etc

These figures help to give some idea of the number of ships that were available in those early days. But the past is brought right into the present in No. 4 prison's cockloft where it is still possible to see ships' timbers used in the original construction. Through the years, prisoners, both French and American, have added holes to take the hammock lashings and have driven nails into beams for hammock supports. Some of these old hammock lashings were still present during the author's first visit in 1969.

In 1971 D2 prison, now F-wing, had a new roof fitted and these beautiful old pitch pine ships' timbers supplied by the docks, thus averting the collapse of the whole project, were removed and taken to the prison quarry. There they still lie thirty years later, open to the elements, quietly rotting away. It is sad to think that these timbers once sailed the oceans of the world, had been involved in sea battles and, having been broken up for use in the prisons, still had usefulness. Here they had character of their own. Each beam bears marks made by the prisoners as they carved pockets in which to hide items or hammered in nails or pieces of bone from which to hang oil lamps. The oil lamps left their own scorch marks on the beams. In No. 4 war prison the beams are still as the French and Americans left them in 1815, some are studded with bones with cloth wrapped around them (photo below left), pieces of uniform perhaps, which prevented the hammock ties fraying.

Roof timbers removed from war prison No. 1 (now F-wing) in 1971 and stored in the prison quarry; an ignoble end to these historic timbers.

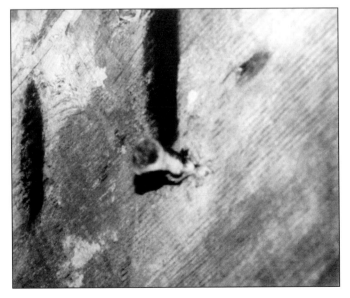

The contractor, who was still struggling to complete the work, wrote in November 1805, 'This hath been a hindering week, the sun hath scarcely made an appearance and £120 had been lost in wages.' Anyone familiar with weather conditions at the prison can vouch for the fact that it is not uncommon for fog and drizzle to descend for up to six weeks at a time.

In 1807 the contractor informed the Admiralty that the road from Roborough to the war prisons had become impassable because of excessive wear from horse-and-cart and other traffic. All that was suggested in return was that the contractor should lay an indictment against the way wardens for repairs. This was to happen again in 1853. In September 1807 the Transport Board of the Admiralty visited to inspect the construction work carried out so far. They reported that: the walls had been poorly built, the chimneys smoked in the houses, there was no heating in the prisons, the steps leading up to the battlements which held the sentry boxes were loose, and that the lime flooring had blistered. This could have been due to too much haste in slaking the lime and unsatisfactory lime being produced, a common fault during the author's time in the building trade.

All of the walls needed pointing to prevent the ingress of water through the bedding joints which could result in destruction through freeze-thaw action. The state of things was wholly unsatisfactory during this time. Tall granite walls simply cannot be built during wet weather. Mortar must always hold the correct amount of water, if it holds too much as a result of heavy rain, then the stones will float and the wall will belly out.

Alexander had promised the Admiralty that the buildings would be ready by Christmas in 1807, about twenty-one months after work had commenced. But the inspection in 1807 stated that the prison could not yet be occupied. The prison buildings were not finished and neither were the barracks for the military guards.

Chapter Two
THE FIRST FRENCH

All of the defects to the buildings discovered during the 1807 inspection were to be rectified and though pressure was put on the contractors to complete the work, it was not until May 1809 that the prisons finally approached completion. The following list shows the first staff appointments at the Dartmoor Depot, as it was then called:

Captain Cotgrave as agent
William Dykar as surgeon
William Dickson as assistant surgeon
1 dispenser
3 hospital mates
1 matron
1 seamstress
1 steward
1 first clerk
1 stores clerk
1 market clerk
1 extra clerk
10 turnkeys
3 labourers
1 foreman of works
1 plumber
1 carpenter
1 mason
1 slater
1 blacksmith
1 navigator [surveyor?]

There were also over 500 military guards housed in the barracks adjoining the prison, with their officers being housed in the army officers' mess. The decision was finally made to occupy the nearly completed war prisons.

Painting by Prison Officer Paul Deacon showing French prisoners being marched up to the Dartmoor Depot, May 1809.

The author beside another painting by Paul Deacon of the French being marched up to the Dartmoor Depot.

On 24 May 1809 a first draft of 2500 French prisoners of war marched to the depot from the hulks at Plymouth. They were moved into the newly built, cold and wet war prisons. The troops themselves were housed in the equally damp and inhospitable barracks Nos 1 to 11. By the end of June 1809 there were 5000 prisoners of war being held at Dartmoor.

WATER SUPPLIES

The water supply to the war prisons was, of course, crucial and in the event was to serve well from 1809 until the 1990s when it was disconnected. Spriddle Lake is a tributary of the River Walkham, OS map reference SX585 803, about four miles from the war prisons. A water course was surveyed and built, finishing up at the reservoir on the highest part of the prison, outside the gates. It is marked on Ordnance Survey maps as the 'prison leat' or 'aqueduct'.

From the reservoir outside the prison gates, water was fed into the round water tower, inside which were five bibcocks A – E which controlled the water, as required, into five open leats. These leats then flowed to different areas in the prison.

Plan of the water tower outside the main prison gate.

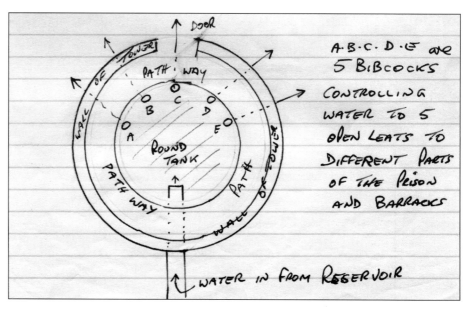

Bibcock A fed the infirmary (now the workshops) and war prisons Nos 1, 2 and 3. Bibcock B fed the surgeon's house, the porters, the reservoir near the marketplace and the cooks. This avoided all buildings and ensured that clean water was available at all times. Bibcock C fed No. 4 war prison and the bathing place for privates and ordinary seamen. D fed the stewards' houses and the military prison for soldiers. It also fed the petty officers' bathing place and prison, and No. 5 war prison. Bibcock E was the overflow to the governor's house and gardens. It then fed through Governor's Field (behind present Burrator Avenue) to the military barracks outside the prison. It passed through the garden of present No. 8 Woodville Avenue and finally to the overflow into the Blackabrook river.

These leats, piped from the water tower, went through the end of each war prison and underneath each privy. As soon as the leat passed out of the end of the first war prison it became the foul leat so a fresh supply went from leat B direct to the cook's supply. This was clean water at all times. The foul leats joined up at the lowest end of the prisons, near the east guardhouse, and became a common foul leat. The location of the foul leat exit was between war prisons Nos 4 and 5. This is where E-wing now stands.

E-wing was built on the site of the old bathing place and it is a strong possibility that the old overflow from the bathing place still exists as E-wing basement floods during heavy rainfall. The old leats collect the rain water. As soon as the foul leat left the prison it went due south to collect the foul effluent from the old prison slaughterhouse (now the site of the prison officers' school built in 1874). There would be a huge quantity of foul to collect from the slaughterhouse because at its peak there were perhaps 10 500 prisoners plus about 1500 troops and members of staff. It took many sheep, pigs and cows to feed 12 000 men.

Top: *The water feed to living areas. A slate was used to skim rubbish off the top of the water.*
Left and above: *Show how the roof was built over the leat, with water still running in this leat today.*

Having collected the foul from the slaughterhouse, the leat proceeded to Thomas Tyrwhitt's leasehold farm at Tor Royal and was distributed over his land below a hill called Broken Barrow. In the lease the foul leat was described to be irrigating Tyrwhitt's land. The final part of the foul leat on prison land, nearest its exit from the war prisons, was filled in by contractors laying new drains in the 1980s. When the war prisons were in full use a large amount of sewage was available for use by Thomas Tyrwhitt.

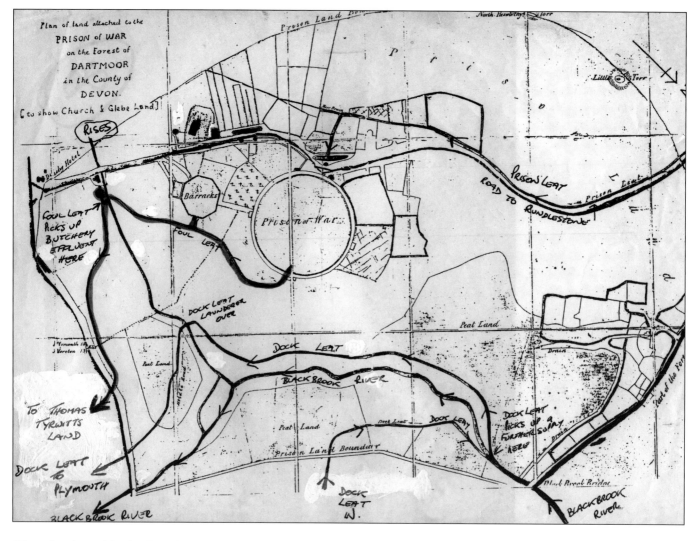

Plan showing glebe land and water courses on the estates: prison leat at top, foul leat in the middle, and Dock Leat and the Blackabrook river at the bottom.

MILITIA

The prison-ship guards at Plymouth were militia men and would have been sent to and from the Dartmoor Depot war prisons on a regular basis to prevent fraternisation with the prisoners of war. For example, in February 1811 the Notts. Regiment of Militia was at the Dartmoor Depot and, as shown on the following list, was on the prison ships in May 1811. Similarly, the Roscommon Regiment of Militia was on the prison ships in February 1812 and at the Dartmoor Depot a little while later. Many regiments of militia served at Dartmoor during its time as a war prison, and a number of those on the following list would have been based at the barracks there:

Prison-ship guards in Plymouth:

1801 September	*Second Royal Veteran Battalion*
1808 August	*First Lancs. Regiment of Militia*
1809 May	*Second Royal Veteran Battalion*
1809 June	*Royal Marines [Second Royal Veteran Battalion ordered to embark for Madeira]*
1809 July	*Second Battalion of Third Regiment of Foot [The Buffs]*
1809 September	*West Essex Regiment of Militia*
1809 November	*First Somerset Regiment of Militia*
1809 December	*First Somerset Regiment of Militia*
1810 February	*First Devon Regiment of Militia*
1810 August	*First Devon Regiment of Militia*
1811 March	*Shropshire Regiment of Militia*
1811 May	*Notts. Regiment of Militia*

1811 June	*First Somerset Regiment of Militia*
1812 January	*First Somerset Regiment of Militia*
1812 February	*Roscommon Regiment of Militia*
1812 March	*Royal South Gloucester Regiment of Militia*
1812 August	*Royal Marines* [short period]
1812 August (end)	*Shropshire Regiment of Militia*
1812 October	*Shropshire Regiment of Militia*
1813 April	*Roscommon Regiment of Militia* [who were to return to Ireland at the end of duty]
1813 April	*Royal Marines*
1813 June	*Hereford and Norfolk Regiment of Militia*
1813 July	*Edinburgh Regiment of Militia* [who embarked and sailed to Ireland at end of duty]
1813 October	*First Somerset Regiment of Militia*
1815 April	*First Somerset Regiment of Militia* [who were on duty on 6 April 1815 on the occasion of the massacre of the American prisoners of war]

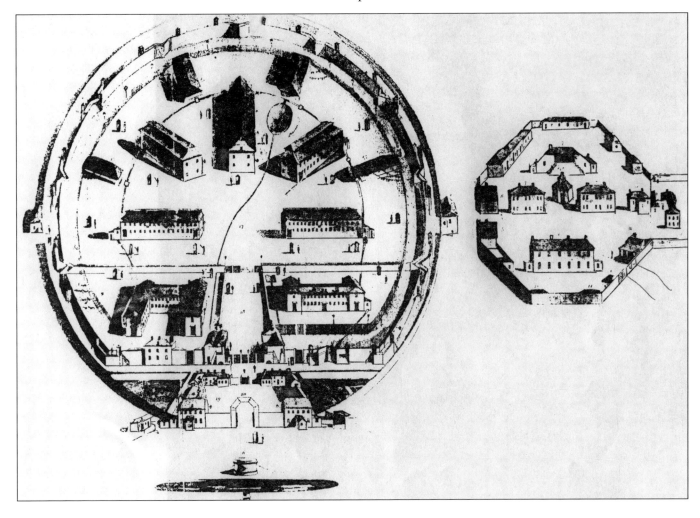

Dartmoor Depot c.1809–12, showing the 11 adjoining barracks.

The short periods of duty continued until the closure of the prison. The military man in charge at Plymouth until 1812 was Lt General R. England who died in London at the end of that year. The Royal Artillery sent detachments of gunners at various intervals throughout the history of the war prison, one of which stayed until the departure of the Americans in 1815, perhaps to back up the militia regiments. A tremendous amount of organisation was needed in order to rotate successfully the militia guards, as all the necessary equipment would have to be moved ahead of each changeover.

More and more French prisoners were being sent to Dartmoor so that by the end of June 1809, just after the first French had been moved in, the roll stood at over 5000 and the supposed maximum of prisoners had already been reached. Five war prisons had been built, each with three floors. The ground floor and the first floor were designed to hold 1000 men. The top floor was, as mentioned before, the cockloft.

The cockloft was used to house prisoners during times of serious overcrowding and in 1812 two extra war prisons were built by the French prisoners. These prisons would later been known as Nos 2 and 6 and were of a slightly different design from the other buildings. The French prisoners who built the extra accommodation were the last to return to their own buildings each evening, having worked the maximum time possible, and once there would be hard-pressed to find a space to sleep.

No. 4 war prison cockloft showing entrance door.

The estimated greatest number of prisoners held was 1500 men to each prison (though figures of 1760 per prison exist). This multiplied by the seven prisons now built, plus a large number of prisoners in the petty officers' prison, perhaps 1000 men, plus the infirmary, would have led to a total of 11–12 000 prisoners being held during the worst periods. It is impossible to be exact about the numbers as men were sent to and received from the hulks, while some were sent home to France and some released on parole to the parole towns.

In 1811 when there were only five war prisons, the roll was 6329 men which was an average of 1265 prisoners per building. With other men housed in the petty officers' prison and the infirmary the prison was obviously overcrowded.

The French in the war prison settled in very well and formed themselves into separate groups according to their social status. These groups were as follows:

Les Lords: Well-to-do men of wealth whose families kept them supplied with money to ease their burden of imprisonment. They were well used to having servants.
Les Indifferents: Described by some as, 'They toil neither do they spin'. They did not bother to make objects to sell in the market to supplement the small allowance provided by the Government. They were well satisfied with their lot.
Les Laborieux: The industrialists who earned money by making and selling objects in the market. These were usually beautiful objects such as ships and other ornaments carved from bone.
Les Minables: Hopeless gamblers who lived only for cards, games of chance and dice.
Les Romains: Also gamesters, but these men sold their clothing and went naked. Even prepared to sell their food to satisfy their passion, they were the most lowly group, with a way of life that was utterly revolting. 'The Romans' were at the very bottom of the league as far as behaviour and conforming was concerned, troublesome in every way.

In 1812 'The Romans' were at last confined to No. 4 prison in a bid to stop the spread of their behaviour. This worked inasmuch as it isolated the problem to one area. They were still in No. 4 prison when the Americans arrived in 1813, living like animals, scouring the garbage heaps for offal or anything else that could be eaten. Finally, in desperation, an inquiry was held in 1813 into their way of life, headed by General Stephenson and Mr Hawker of Plymouth. Subsequently a letter from the Transport Board was sent to Captain E. Hawkins RN, superintendent of hulks at Plymouth:

> *Sir,*
> *500 prisoners are coming from Dartmoor and 500 are to be returned to Dartmoor from Mill Prison, these coming from Dartmoor are sent because of selling of their clothes etc and are to be put in the prison ship.*

On 16 October 1813 a ragged mob of 436 of 'The Romans' were scrubbed, dressed and placed under a strong guard, then marched to the hulks at Plymouth. There they were held under fearsome discipline until hostilities ended. So ended *Les Romains'* reign at Dartmoor. Incredibly, some of these fearsome and revolting men, on their return to France, became respectable citizens and even reached high office in life.

The war prisons housed more than 10 000 men including the staff. They all had to be fed and watered, along with a garrison of 500 troops. By the time the Americans arrived there would be more than 1000 troops at the prison. A slaughterhouse was opened in the village of Princetown on the site of what is now the village school. The stream, now called Moor Brook, runs down to the Blackabrook river past the butchery building, and so a supply of fresh water was taken from the brook into the butchery. After it had been used, the water was diverted into the foul leat that carried sewage from the war prisons to Tyrwhitt's land.

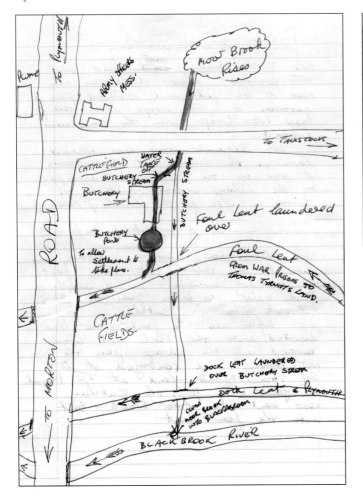

Left: *The author's sketch showing the prison butchery, and its take-off from the Moor Brook for use in the butchery. A foul outlet then joined the prison foul leat for discharge on Thomas Tyrwhitt's land.*
Above: *Workmen uncover a typical water leat on prison land.*

IRON RATIONS

It is interesting to compare the rations of food for Dartmoor Prison with those in France that housed English prisoners of war. Taking just one French example, Pontanezan Prison, where the food was reported as very poor: one day's ration comprised 16 ounces of biscuit of a bad quality and mouldy, two ounces of rotten fat, beef or pork, and pease soup made up from hot water plus a few horse peas. Many prisoners became extremely ill and died, attributed to the copper cooking vessels becoming contaminated. No cleaning was carried out so such poisoning was prevalent.

Prisoners were robbed of all their possessions, including their clothes. Exchanges of war prisoners took place but these were usually in favour of the French. Exchanges at one period saw 5045 men being sent back to France while only 2995 English were received.

At Dartmoor the rations were supplied daily in messes of six men to a container. Each man received one quart of beer, 1½ pounds of bread, ⅓ ounce of salt and ¾ pound of beef, except on Saturdays when 4 ounces of butter or 6 ounces of cheese were substituted. This was over 3 tons of beef per day. They were also given ½ pint of peas on four days of the week.

The bedding supplied at Dartmoor comprised one hammock, one palliasse, one bolster and one blanket. The straw in the palliasse was to be changed as often as occasion required. Men were also issued with clothing which consisted of a hat, jacket, waistcoat, trousers, shirt, shoes, stockings and a handkerchief.

On 8 October 1812 the prison bakehouse burned down. Contractors had to send in bread but at first the prisoners refused to eat it as they deemed it inferior to prison bread. Apparently this is the case even today. During heavy snowfall which blocked the roads to the prison, staff were allowed to purchase prison-baked bread. It was beautifully crusty and in great demand!

Undoubtedly, the outside contractors cheated whenever they could so it was arranged that the agent, surgeon, first clerk and two prisoners from each of the five war prisons would inspect the bread as it arrived. It was tasted by all of the men to see that it met the contract specifications. On 9 March 1813 the whole of the batch provided by Gill & Hornbrook of Tavistock was rejected and sent back to the bakery. This was despite the fact that back in 1812 Phillip Thorne and Thomas Parry of Tavistock had come forward and proved cheating on the part of a Tavistock baker called Twynan, resulting in the contractors being sentenced to imprisonment for their cheating.

Phillip Thorne also gave testimony against Gill & Hornbrook but demanded too much money for his informing on this occasion and the Admiralty decided not to proceed. As late as 1819, three years after the prison had closed, Richard Fox, another informer, was complaining to the Admiralty that the evidence which he had given six years before in 1813 had ruined him. He had to live among the people of Tavistock who did not like informers. He went to work for the Admiralty as nobody else would employ him.

Chapter Three

LIFE IN THE WAR PRISONS

The petty officers' prison was known as *'le petit cautionnement'* (the little parole). It held naval and merchant navy officers who had forfeited their parole by misconduct or attempting to escape. Some were professional men such as lawyers, doctors, artists, musicians, and apparently even a Black general who had served under Rochambeau but could not obtain parole because of the colour of his skin.

The plan of the war prisons below shows the PO prison (No. 15) self contained within its own grounds. This was an area in which the men could freely roam, included a bathing place, an open-air pond fed by a leat from the water tower outside the gates. These PO grounds were the same as war prisons Nos 1 to 7 as regards security and supervision. Around the grounds were ramparts for the military guards armed with muskets. Inside the ramparts a boundary was marked by a wicker fence and railings, six inches apart and only three feet high, but these could not be crossed for fear of a musket shot ringing about one's ears.

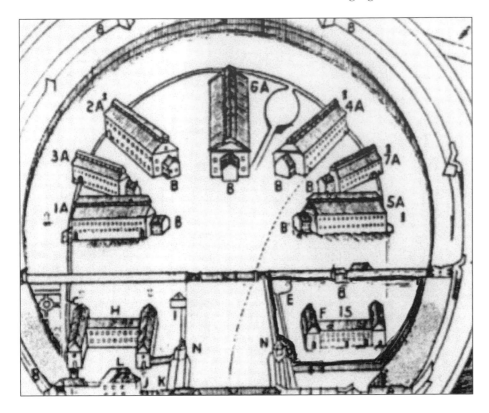

A contemporary plan of the seven war prisons incorporates a somewhat confusing numbering system. Later each war prison block was referred to from No. 1 through to No. 7 clockwise.

Due to their high rank and wealth, those held in the PO prison were allowed to employ subordinate prisoners to act as servants. Officers and petty officers could draw money from their bankers through London agents to pay their servants, who earned about 3d. per day. This was a high rate of pay for duties no more onerous than those performed in service in the outside world. The officers enjoyed a very leisurely imprisonment.

An extension to the hospital, built in 1912, incorporated an archway that was originally part of the petty officers' prison.

The petty officers' prison today.

War prison No. 6 as built in 1812 by French prisoners of war. In the 1940s the roof of this famous old building was lowered and it was converted into the prison kitchen and used until the 1990s when a new kitchen was built at the bottom of the marketplace.

The seven war prisons were self-governing to a point. They could each elect a *'commissaire de salle'* who acted as governor for the war prison. He also acted as a magistrate who could award punishment to prisoners who broke the rules. These commissaires were responsible to the president, a French prisoner who was in charge of all commissaires, and, of course, responsible to Captain Cotgrave, the prison agent. Later Cotgrave was replaced by Captain Shortland who remained in charge until 1816 when the prisons closed.

The war prisons were similar to the 'stalags' of the Third Reich in the Second World War, with English officers responsible for the day-to-day running of the stalags, and an officer responsible for German command.

Movement anywhere within the grounds of the war prison was permitted but not beyond the iron railings overlooked by the sentries. The prison buildings were unlocked at dawn and the prisoners counted, then not locked again until dusk. The counting routine was particularly arduous for those who were sick, as every man was required to parade outside his war prison each morning. As it took at least one hour to get the men lined up in ranks to count them, and more than 1500 men were in each prison, some of the prisoners collapsed and died in the cold. On Captain Shortland taking over from Cotgrave on 22 December 1813, this cruel parade at first light was abandoned, to be held later in the day. Even so the French had to endure it for four years prior to this.

The provision of food in the war prisons was not always considered adequate by the inmates and those men who could not buy extra provisions in the market went hungry. This led, unsurprisingly, to trouble flaring up, with fights breaking out among the prisoners due to their pent-up feelings. These fights, often taking the form of duels, resulted in an increasing number of deaths. Eventually the combined death toll, including that from suicide and illness, sparked a protest from the Plymouth coroner who stated that the inquests in a single year at the war prisons had exceeded all the inquests for the previous fourteen years combined.

In February 1810 Mr White, the coroner for Plymouth, complained about the burden thrown upon the parish in respect of juries summoned for inquests upon French prisoners 'who have laid violent hands upon themselves or have been otherwise killed'. The Admiralty, in a bid to overcome the problem of shortage of money, decided to pay 50 per cent more to each juror, increasing the pay from 8d. to 1s. for each inquest.

A typical duel occurred on August 1809 when the French prisoners decided to hold a procession, headed by a band. When the parade was organised a prisoner named Sarville, a forty-year-old who had served three years in another English prison, decided it was unjust that a young man of eighteen should be awarded the great honour of carrying the flag of his country. The young man resisted Sarville's attempt to get the banner from him and gave him a hiding in a fist fight. Immediately Sarville challenged him to a duel. Inexperienced in such things, the younger man decided that in order to protect his life the duel should be with razor blades mounted on long sticks. As combat began, he rushed at the experienced Sarville who, using a well-aimed stroke, slashed the young lad's hand. As soon as blood was shed the duel was ended by the seconds.

In June 1814 a duel between two highly experienced fencing masters ended in death. It started, as so often, very simply. A few heated words on the merits of their respective pupils led to a fist fight in which a Frenchman by the name of Jean Vignon got the worst of it. He challenged his opponent to a contest of small arms but the other man at first declined saying that he would fight no duels in a prison. Vignon must have been a persuasive man because next morning the pair were seen to go up the stairs to the cockloft of No. 4 prison with their swords. An American prisoner found them there. Vignon was standing with his sword in his hand while his opponent was stooping to pick up his weapon. At this moment Vignon thrust with his sword and his opponent fell mortally wounded. Vignon later expressed regret for his actions but in August that year he was tried for manslaughter at Exeter assizes. Found guilty, Vignon was sentenced to six months' imprisonment.

Above: *The cockloft in war prison No. 4 in which carvings made by French prisoners of war can still be seen.*
Right: *A lead cross placed on No. 1 war prison (now F-wing) commemorates a French prisoner shot dead by a sentry.*

Regulations which all prisoners of war are bound to observe.

I. All orders given by the Agent who may have the superintendence of the prisoners, or by any other officer belonging to the prison, shall be attended to and immediately executed by the prisoners without any dispute, reply or hesitation whatever.

The prisoners are forbidden to strike or even to menace or insult any officer, turnkey or other person employed in the prison, under the pain of losing their turn of exchange, of being closely confined in the cachot and forfeiting one-third of their ration, or suffering such other punishment as the Commissioners may think proper to direct.

II. The prisoners are strictly forbidden to fight, quarrel or excite any tumult or disorder in the prison, or in the places where they may be allowed to take the air, under pain of being confined in the cachot, or forfeiting one-third of their ration for a time proportioned to the offence.

III. All the prisoners shall answer to their call at the muster whenever the Agent shall direct, and if there shall be any error in the list delivered to the Agent, they shall point it out to prevent the confusion which might arise from any mistake in the name, and any prisoners who shall refuse to answer to his call shall be deprived of his ration until he shall submit.

IV. The prison shall be swept, scraped and washed by the prisoners in rotation as often and in such manner as the Agent shall order, and any prisoner who shall refuse to perform this service in his turn after having been warned of it shall be deprived of his ration until he shall comply. One prisoner out of every six shall be employed in this service, and during the time that they shall be employed in cleaning the prison, all the prisoners except those who shall be so employed at the moment must quit the apartment or room of the prison.

V. If any damage should be done to the prison in which prisoners are kept, either in their attempts to escape or by design, all the prisoners in the room where the damage may have been done shall be put on two-thirds rations until, by such deduction, the expense of repairing the damage shall be made good.

VI. Any prisoner who shall be taken attempting to escape shall be put in the cachot for ten days and shall lose his turn of exchange, and any prisoner who shall be retaken after having escaped from the prison, and shall by this means have occasioned expenses, shall not only lose his turn of exchange and be put in the cachot, but shall, with the whole of the prisoners kept in the same room from which he has escaped, be reduced to two-thirds of their ration until by such deduction the expenses shall be made good; and even if he shall not be retaken, the whole of the prisoners are in the same manner to reimburse such expense.

VII. A market is allowed to be held in each prison from nine o'clock in the morning till twelve on every day except Sunday, that such prisoners as have the means may be enabled to purchase such articles or clothes as they may wish for, and the Agent and officers will take care that the prisoners are not imposed upon in the prices, but the prisoners are forbidden to buy or to introduce into the prison liquors, knives or weapons of any kind under pain of being confined in the cachot for ten days for each offence.

VIII. The prisoners are allowed during market hours to sell articles of their own manufacture, except mittens or woollen gloves, straw hats or bonnets, shoes, plaited straw, obscene pictures or images and articles formed out of the prison stores, which are all strictly forbidden, and any prisoner making or selling any of these forbidden articles, or found to have any of such articles in his possession, shall be confined to the cachot and reduced to two-thirds rations for three days, and such prohibited articles as are found shall be destroyed.

IX. Each prisoner shall receive a ticket from the Agent specifying the different articles which have been delivered to him, and on failure of producing this ticket when asked for it by the Agent, he shall be confined in the cachot and reduced to two-thirds rations for three days.

X. If any prisoner shall steal, deliberately and designedly damage, or buy, sell, or otherwise make away with the coverlets, hammocks, or other articles of bedding, or other articles belonging to the prison, all the prisoners in the same room shall be reduced to two-thirds of their ration until by such reduction the damaged or lost articles be replaced, and the offenders shall lose their turn of exchange.

XI. Any prisoner who shall have bought, sold or disposed of his ration by gambling or otherwise, or shall have sold or made away with any article of clothing, even though such article belong to him, he shall be confined in the cachot and shall receive only two-thirds of his ration during such time as the Agent shall direct, and he shall lose his turn of exchange.

XII. Any prisoner who shall offer, or propose to buy the turn of exchange of a fellow-prisoner, or shall sell or propose to sell his turn of exchange under any consideration or in any way whatever, shall infallibly lose his turn of exchange, and in all cases the buyer and seller shall be considered equally culpable.

XIII. All letters sent by prisoners, or addressed to them, must pass through the Agent's hands for the purpose of being examined by him, and if any attempts are made to send letters through any other channel, such letters, being discovered, shall be destroyed, and the writers of them, as well as such prisoners as attempted to pass them out of the prison, shall be punished in such a way as the Agent shall direct.

XIV. In each prison the prisoners are to name three or five from among them to examine the provisions furnished by the contractor for the purpose of giving their opinion whether the articles are good, and whether they have their regular allowance conformably with the undermentioned table of rations, with a surplus of 5 lbs. for each cwt. of beef, and 2 lbs. for each cwt. of bread each day, and if it shall appear to the prisoners appointed for this purpose that there is any cause of complaint with regard to the said provisions, or in any other case whatsoever, they are respectfully to inform the Agent, who will remedy it if the complaint is well founded.

XV. The prisoners will receive their rations in messes of six men each, and every mess is to name a chief who shall be responsible for the bowl, the wooden dish, the can, and the pot and spoons furnished to each mess, and he is also required to be present when the rations of each mess are given out.

XVI. If it is found that any prisoner has escaped and that the others belonging to the same mess have nevertheless received the same rations without having informed the Agent or one of the clerks or turnkeys of the escape of such prisoner, all the other prisoners belonging to the same mess shall be reduced to two-thirds allowance for the space of ten days.

XVII. A certain number of prisoners are to be nominated by the Agent as inspectors for the preservation of good order and to see that the established regulations of the prison are attended to, and at the same time to inform the Agent if any of the prisoners shall misbehave.

XVIII. Some of the prisoners shall be employed in the capacity of barbers to shave the prisoners, and it is particularly recommended to the prisoners to pay every possible attention to personal cleanliness, as this is of the greatest importance for the preservation of their health.

Regulations with which prisoners had to comply, drawn up by the Transport Board, taken from Governor Thompson's book Dartmoor Prison.

To maintain discipline and make the prisoners comply with the foregoing regulations, punishment awarded within the petty officers' prison for the worst offenders was expulsion from their comfortable quarters and transfer to one of the ordinary war prisons, a distinct lowering of lifestyle. For those held in war prisons Nos 1 to 7, any misdemeanour meant being incarcerated in the dreaded cachot.

The author's sketch of the cachot (punishment block), taken from the original plans of the war prisons.

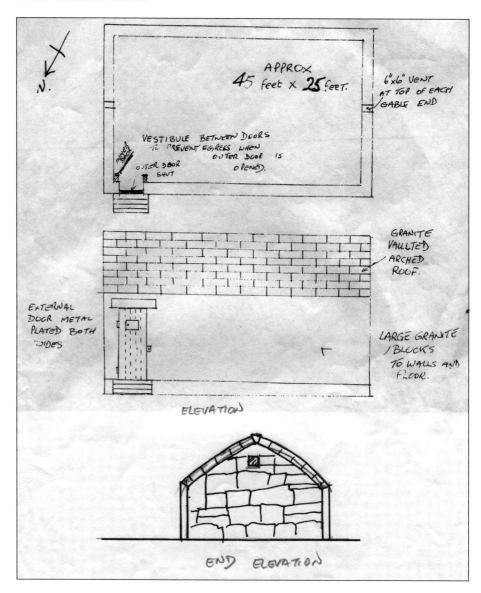

In the early years of the war prisons the cachot was a tiny building made from rough masonry. Prisoners who broke the regulations would be incarcerated within its narrow confines, bereft of light and comfort. Eventually, it was just too small to cope with the large numbers of French (and later, American) prisoners sent there to maintain discipline (today E-wing is used to house miscreants). Early in 1811 the foreman of works, Mr Walters, decided to design and build another, larger, cachot using French labour. This was erected on the site of the present G-wing. Huge granite blocks weighing more than a ton each were laid as a foundation to prevent prisoners from trying to tunnel out. The walls and vaulted roof were constructed from large dressed-granite blocks of a similar size.

The completed building, as shown by a surviving drawing at the prison, was approximately 45 by 25 feet. It had no windows and the only ventilation was through two openings, under the vaulted roof, of about six by four inches. These allowed the stench of foul air to escape. A solid wooden door was plated on both sides with iron sheets and the door had a wicket of about eight inches square to allow food to be passed through to the long-term prisoners.

The cachot no longer exists and the author's sketch is taken from an official plan held at the prison. Other buildings shown on the plan, many of which still exist, enabled the approximate size of the cachot to be estimated.

The floor of the cachot was raw granite. When you place a bare hand against granite it feels intensely cold. The warmth from your body is drawn straight into the stone. Pity then the naked prisoners of war who, in the middle of winter's coldest days, would be kept locked up, hungry and frozen to the marrow, with no beds or chairs. Many were forced to spend long periods in the cachot and many died as a result of their incarceration. Those who did not had to endure the torturous effect of almost total darkness, for the doors were designed to keep out daylight; a terrible place indeed.

In 1811 the French prisoners built an entrance gateway from the exterior barracks into the prison, allowing the troops in the barracks to enter directly on to the military road which circled the prison. The new entrance was called the postern gate, and later, in 1813, a French prisoner called Henri engraved the granite lintel with the following inscription:

HENRI PRISONNIER 1813 JOURNE FRANCAIS

The lintel inscribed by French prisoner 'Henri'.

This has proved to be an enduring memorial to Henri, whoever he was. As the engraved lintel was on the outer face of a wall, overlooked by the muskets from the embattlements on the other side of the military road, perhaps Henri had special permission to make his carving, as no prisoners would have been allowed there otherwise, and would have been shot if discovered.

The French cemetery holds just under 1200 men who would almost all have been fit servicemen on their arrival at Dartmoor. The worst period was between November 1809 and April 1810 when 500 men died, an average of 100 men each month, more than three per day. This mortality would have been due mainly to sickness and is a truly shocking figure. When men died in the infirmary their bodies were taken through a small gate in the iron railings, across an area known as Dead Man's Land close to the second battlements, and through a small gate in the outer boundary wall. This was about 25 paces west of the north guardroom. The men were then buried in shallow graves on the land around the area that is now covered by the former gasworks and farm buildings. The wind and rain soon eroded the sodden peat and the animals grazing on the land, especially pigs, began to expose the bones of the men buried there, leaving them to be bleached by the sun.

Previous mention has been made of the beams in the cockloft above prison No. 4. The cockloft lies above what is now the Church of England chapel. The lamp-burns on the beams are clearly visible. The author often used to spend any free time sitting in the cockloft and contemplating the existence of the prisoners of war who once hung their oil lamps from those beams. One can almost feel their absolute suffering and torment while sitting there. At one time all seven of the prisons had cocklofts but these have all disappeared with demolition and alteration of roof space.

There are also visible remains of where the hammocks would have hung. Holes were cut into the beams for this purpose and large nails were also employed. Even gate-hangers were put to use, hammered into the beams; in fact anything that could be found. In 1992 when the author was last in No. 4 prison cockloft there were nails still wrapped in cloth, used to protect the hammock ties from wearing through.

The entrance to No. 4 cockloft has been built up over many years. When refurbishment was carried out in 1971 the original doorway was uncovered and unfortunately a painter instructed a party of prisoners to scrub the beams and clean the area. All artefacts left by the prisoners of war were removed. These men thought that their work was helpful but to the author it caused inestimable damage to the history of the building. French inscriptions carved into the beams were covered up and hidden behind new ceilings and beam cladding during this refurbishment. A large amount of lime-washing, known as bug-blinding, was also done by the prisoners of war who then carved into the coats of lime. All this was lost.

When the roof space was opened up in 1971, the atmosphere was intense. I will never forget how I felt. A great deal of sadness prevailed in those old ship timbers. So dramatic was the effect of first walking into that cockloft that had a bearded prisoner and a red-coated soldier walked past, I would not have been surprised.

One retired principal officer who has never been into the No. 4 cockloft but has been on the ground floor, in the chapel, felt such a strong presence, even here, that he disliked going into the building alone. The chapel, as well as being used for services, in later years, 1968–80, also saw use as a cinema.

In later years I took a group of Americans, whose ancestors had been held at Dartmoor, into the same cockloft and, again, several of them confided in me that they too had extremely strong feelings about the place.

The French completed building work inside and outside the prison during their incarceration at Dartmoor. Not only did they construct the church and the chaplain's house, they also built a row of eight houses for staff named Church Row. The name was later changed to Chapel Row, presumably at the time when the church became the chapel of ease. It was then changed again to Government Row, when the convict prison opened, and again to Woodville Terrace before being demolished.

The men who worked on the buildings were paid for their labour although if just one man attempted escape this would mean all men would lose three months' pay. At the end of the day the men would march back to the prison where at night a cow's horn was blown to let them know it was time to retire to their hammocks. If anyone left it a little too late, it would have been almost impossible to find the right hammock amidst the seething mass of men. So it was vital for the men to return from labour as quickly as possible or risk sleeping on the hard floor beneath the hammocks amid a sea of humanity. Or should this be inhumanity?

War prison No. 4 cockloft, with the only window at ground level. A few more windows were set at a higher level and this made it impossible for prisoners to see out of the building.

The beams of war prison No. 4 bearing lamp-burns and holes cut for hammock lashings. Sometimes hammocks were tied to nails wrapped with cloth, while the photograph (bottom right) shows a gate-hanger was also used for this purpose. No. 4 cockloft, which held French and American prisoners of war in such terrible conditions, is the only remaining cockloft from the seven war prisons, and is thus of great importance historically.

Chapter Four
VANHILLE'S
LONG WALK

French officers and sometimes petty officers were given the chance for limited liberty in the form of parole. This is still in force today for inmates but, in addition, the French were given an allowance so that they could live reasonably well. Many prisoners were released to local parole towns including Tavistock, Okehampton, Bodmin, Launceston, Moretonhampstead, Ashburton and Callington. The French Marshal, Cambronne, was quartered in the salubrious surroundings of the house of Sergeant Eddy at Ashburton and, for many years, his portrait hung in the town's Golden Lion Hotel.

The paroled prisoners were permitted to walk a maximum of one mile, or 'one miol' as one parole stone states. But many of the favoured officer-class who were released broke parole and escaped to France. If caught they would be returned immediately to the war prisons at Dartmoor and then incarcerated in the petty officers' prison.

Parole stones were placed approximately a mile from parole town's boundaries (in this case Ashburton). The 'J miol' stone can still be seen on the roadside between Widecombe-in-the-Moor and Natsworthy.

The gravestones of two paroled French prisoners in the porch of Widecombe Church.

Paroled prisoners were issued with letters of parole which they had to carry. Similar notices were also posted in the parole towns for townspeople to read. Below is a typical notice:

Whereas the commissioners for conducting His Majesty's Transport Services, and for the care and custody of French officers and sailors detained in England, have been pleased to grant _____ leave to reside in _____ upon condition that he gives his parole of honour not to withdraw one mile from the boundaries prescribed there, without leave for that purpose from the said commissioners.
That he will behave himself decently, and with due regard to the laws of the Kingdom. Also he will not directly or indirectly hold any correspondence with France during his continuance in England, but by such letter or letters as shall be shown to the agent of the said commissioners under his care he is, or maybe in order to them being read and approved by the superiors. He does hereby declare that having been given his parole of honour he will keep it inviolably.
Captain Cotgrave RN Agent

The notices posted in the parole towns read as follows:

Notice is hereby given that all such prisoners are permitted to walk, or ride, on the Great Turnpike Road within the distance of one mile from the extreme parts of the town, not beyond the bounds of the parish, and if they exceed such limits, or go into any field or cross roads, they shall be taken up and sent to prison and a reward of 10s. will be paid by the agent for apprehending him.

And further that such prisoners are to be in their lodgings by five o'clock in the winter, or eight o'clock in the summer months, and if they stay out later they are liable to be taken up and sent to the agent for such misconduct.

And to prevent the prisoners from behaving in an improper manner to the inhabitants of the town, or creating any riots or disturbances either with them or among themselves.

Notice is also given that the commissioners will cause, upon information being given to the agent, any prisoner who shall so misbehave to be committed to prison. And such of the inhabitants who shall insult or abuse and of the prisoners of war on parole, or shall be found in any respect aiding or assisting in the escape of such prisoners shall be prosecuted according to law.

Captain Cotgrave RN Agent Dartmoor Depot

By February 1813 there were 2200 French commissioned officers and 1260 of inferior rank on parole. Presumably these were petty officers. The parole allowance paid to commissioned officers was 1s.6d. per day and petty officers 1s.3d. per day. Complaints about the inadequacy of these allowances were made quite often. On 8 February 1813 M. Rivière of the French Admiralty wrote a letter to the Transport Board pointing out that, although the allowances paid to French prisoners on parole in England were greater than those paid to English officers on parole in France, the allowances were in reality smaller as the cost of living in England was much greater.

The board called upon Lieutenant Wallis, who had recently escaped from France, to check on all items in France and state what an Englishman living in France would require. His figures were then compared with M. Rivière's. Lt Wallis's figures for an Englishman living in France were as follows:

1lb of bread	2d.
1lb of beef	4d.
¾ qt of beer	1d.
Beer/wine taken alternately one per day	5¼d.
Veg and fruit	½d.
Milk	½d.
Cooking expenses	2d.
Total	1s.3¼d. per day

M. Rivière reckoned the cost per day to be only 0.9 pence. According to Lt Wallis a Frenchman living in England required:

¾ loaf of bread	5d.
¾ lb of beef	7½d.
2 qts of beer	6d.
pot of wine	5d.
Veg/apples	2d.
Cooking expenses	2d.
Milk	2d.
Total	2s.5½d. per day

M. Rivière states that the amount required would be 2s. per day. As the allowance was only 1s.6d. and 1s.3d. per day, it seems that M. Rivière proved his case that living in England was twice as expensive as living in France. But there are no records of any changes to the allowance.

An entry in the *Plymouth and Dock Telegraph* on 16 November 1811 reads:

On Tuesday last an officers' guard belonging to the Somerset militia proceeded to Launceston for the purpose of escorting all the French prisoners on parole at that place to the prison at Dartmoor. The number of French prisoners so sent off amounted to 37, their removal to the Dartmoor Depot has been occasioned by the French order to imprison the British prisoners of war in France.

So this was a 'tit-for-tat' episode. There are no records of any other parole town doing the same so perhaps Launceston paid the price for the French action. I wonder whether Launceston was chosen because of the parole exploits of a certain Mr V, whose escape is documented in the plan shown below.

The sketch, by John Wethems, of the plan of the war prison in 1812 shows No. 14 prison where Mr V 'made his first entry' on 12 December 1811. It also shows No. 15 where Mr V 'lives now' and the track of his permitted walk. Finally No. 16 shows where Mr V had the liberty to walk as far as the fifth gate, which is the outer arch gate. It seems astonishing that Mr V had permission to leave the petty officers' prison compound to walk through the Agent's Square as far as the gate which used to stand under the outer arch.

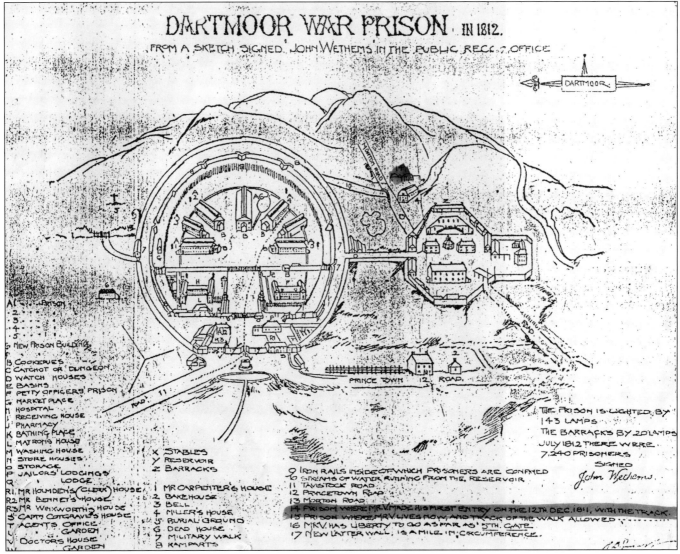

An accurate plan of the Dartmoor Depot, signed by John Wethems, and (top) the outer arch gate to which Mr V was allowed access.

I have always wondered whether Mr V mentioned on the map is actually the M. Vanhille whose extraordinary story is related below, it certainly seems to be feasible when looking at the events surrounding Vanhille.

On 2 May 1806 HMS *Barfleur* and HMS *Druid* captured the French corvette *Le Pandour* of which Vanhille was commissary. Vanhille was born in Dunkirk, on 6 March 1780 making him twenty-six years old when captured. He is described as a stout man (meaning muscular), about five and a half feet tall, with light brown hair, grey eyes and a fresh complexion. He looked like an Englishman and, indeed, spoke English very well.

Following his capture, Vanhille spent a week at Mill Prison in Plymouth from where he was granted parole and taken to Launceston in the care of a brewer named John Tyeth whose address was Brick Lane, Launceston. Mr Tyeth was a Nonconformist with five daughters, two of whom were married to local preachers in Cornwall. The family was extremely respectable.

Vanhille soon became involved with Tyeth's youngest daughter, Fanny, to whom he was supposed to be engaged. He also became close to a fellow lodger and Frenchman, a surgeon named Dr Deronge. Although prisoners on parole were permitted to walk a mile from the parole town, Vanhille soon began to walk further and further, venturing way beyond the one-mile limit set by the parole board. Stephen Spetigue, who was the parole officer for Launceston, apparently did not supervise the prisoners in his area very efficiently.

Vanhille and other prisoners continued to push further and further beyond the parole limits, even including himself in a shooting party near Tavistock and attending the Bodmin races! One must remember that in these days the Cornish had few kind feelings towards being English and perhaps had some sympathy for the French in their fight against England.

At this time the niece of Mr Digory Bray, an auctioneer in Launceston, gave birth to a child. She said that the father was Dr Deronge, the French prisoner, although he vehemently denied it. The overseer of Launceston parish gave a judgement of £25 against Deronge, who was unable to pay, and so Vanhille paid the money for him. The embarrassing publicity led to an inquiry into the whole matter and Spetigue, perhaps eager to save his job, detained Vanhille and Deronge and charged them with breaking the one-mile rule in order to dine with Alderman Mabyn of Camelford. As a result they both forfeited parole and on 12 December 1811 were sent to Dartmoor Depot. Vanhille had missed the mass transfer of parolees from Launceston back to Dartmoor in November 1811, perhaps thanks to the influence of the notable people he was acquainted with in Cornwall.

Vanhille spent about ten months at Dartmoor until, on 22 August 1812, he failed to answer his name on roll call. The prison then knew that they had 'one away'. It was discovered much later that Vanhille had made his way to Bristol, more than 100 miles away, sailing from there to the New World on a vessel named *Jane*.

The *Jane* landed at Montego Bay in Jamaica on 4 February 1813 after a long Atlantic crossing. The boarding officer reported to the magistrates that among the passengers was a character named Williams who could not give a satisfactory account of his business there. He was arrested as a spy and his papers were checked. Vanhille then admitted his identity and said that he was hoping to make it to the French Quarter of New Orleans in America where his brother lived.

Unfortunately Vanhille had too much of a methodical mind for his own good. All of his papers were completely up to date and recorded his every movement since leaving Dartmoor. His personal documents such as his birth certificate were in his possession, along with a plan of England showing his travels and where he had stopped. He also carried letters of credit from one of his correspondents in England, a tailor from Launceston by the name of John Rowe. All of these papers were impounded in the hope of discovering how he had escaped from Dartmoor, perhaps to find whether he had been assisted by treasonable Englishmen.

Vanhille was again sent back to Dartmoor aboard a Royal Navy frigate and was put into the prison hulk *Krown Prince* at Chatham on 22 June 1813. The Transport Board was now in possession of all Vanhille papers and they began a thorough investigation that was to reveal the incredible story of Vanhille's escapades. Firstly papers were sent to Messrs Eastlake, solicitors of Plymouth, who in turn contacted an exciseman by the name of Beale. He was a private agent who carried out further investigation into the whole business, having known Deronge and Vanhille in Launceston.

It seemed that Vanhille and Deronge had conned Tyeth and his two daughters, the postmistresses at Launceston. They in turn had obtained assistance from John Rowe, a tailor, who supplied clothing and letters of credit, a Mrs Miller who bought and sold poultry at Plymouth market, Digory Penwarden, a Tavistock ironmonger, and Mary Ellis who had a donkey and visited the marketplace at Dartmoor Depot twice a week. It was this motley crew who aided Vanhille's escape.

On 7 August Mary Ellis brought clothes to the market, apparently supplied by John Rowe the tailor, hidden under the cover of her skirts. These clothes were handed to Vanhille who changed into them and then walked out of the prison with Mary Ellis when the bell sounded to close the market. On walking out of the prison dressed as a Devonshire wagoner, Vanhille walked through Tavistock to Launceston where he spent the night with his old friends the Tyeths. The next day he walked to Camelford and met Alderman Mabyn who told him that 'as a friend I am happy to see you but you cannot stay under my roof'. Bearing in mind Mabyn knew very well that Vanhille was an escaped prisoner of war, this is astonishing and reveals the tremendous sympathy shown to the French prisoners at this time.

Vanhille then set off for St Columb, next day taking the ferry at Padstow and sleeping at St Teath. He could not find a ship leaving for a foreign port so he took a stage wagon back to Launceston. Here he met Tyeth who arranged that Vanhille could stay with his brother, the rector of St Stephen's.

Tyeth gave money to Vanhille who then set off on the long trek to the port of Bideford in North Devon where he awaited passage aboard a ship to Newport in South Wales, just across the Bristol Channel from Bideford. Vanhille returned in the same vessel to Appledore, along the estuary from Bideford, but on 8 September was back in Cornwall at Launceston again. His hope was that all these wanderings would throw the authorities off the scent. The fact that none of the people in all the areas he visited gave the game away reflects the general opinion of the English towards the French prisoners of war.

Vanhille soon left Launceston en route to London, travelling via Okehampton, Exeter and Salisbury. He spent two days in London then on 15 September left for Petersfield via Guildford. From Guildford he returned via Winchester and on 20 September reached Bristol where he embarked on the *New Passage* for Usk, travelling then to Abergavenny. He then returned in the same vessel and travelled, yet again, all the way back to Launceston where he spent a week with the Tyeth family.

Vanhille visited most of the parole towns in the south of England without being challenged. He was known in many places but still nobody turned him in. On 5 October 1813 Vanhille walked to Falmouth carrying papers forged by the Tyeths. He spent two nights at Falmouth, at the Blue Anchor, but he unfortunately could not find any vessel bound for America where his brother lived. Once again he returned to Launceston where he was supplied with funds and a bible by Tyeth, then set off once more on the long trek back to Bristol.

Vanhille waited three weeks in Bristol before securing passage for Jamaica on the *Jane*. Bad weather delayed the ship and he arrived at Cork in southern Ireland too late to catch the convoy to America – the war requiring ships to travel together for protection. He had to wait until 19 December before the next convoy of 80 vessels had been gathered for passage to the West Indies. During the delay he again contacted the Tyeths and, with the postmistresses' collusion, was sent a box of clothing. Tyeth, of course, wrote in a disguised hand.

In a little over two months after escaping from Dartmoor with the help of his English friends, Vanhille had travelled more than 1230 miles in England, mostly on foot. It seems amazing that an escaped prisoner of war managed to evade capture so easily. But what of all the people who assisted him in his escape?

Tyeth the brewer in Launceston, as a future father-in-law to Vanhille, did his utmost to ensure the Frenchman evaded capture. John Rowe, the tailor, only wanted business for his tailor's shop and, after all, tailors were permitted to sell clothing to French prisoners at the depot market. He admitted signing a letter of credit but the jury at Exeter found him not guilty of assisting in the escape. Tyeth's brother had housed Vanhille after his escape but this could not be proved by the prosecutors. The exciseman Beale, who did all the investigation into the Vanhille affair, reported the following, 'I find nothing to be done to the Launcestonians, they all hang together in knavery'.

A cartel left for Calais, France, on 19 May 1814 carrying a number of French prisoners of war back to their home country. Vanhille was among them and so at last he made it back to his beloved France, leaving his fellow prisoners to remain at Dartmoor for almost a further two years.

A building at Ockery, known as Trena Bridge on prison maps. This would have been a site well known to French prisoners, such as Vanhille, as it was only a little distance from the prison.

Vanhille's story is told in full in *Dartmoor Prison* by Basil Thompson who was able to refer to prison records which were later lost in the fire caused by the 1932 mutiny.

ESCAPE AND PUNISHMENT

There were many attempted escapes during the time of the war prisons, the first occurring just five days after the initial batch of 2500 French prisoners had arrived at the depot. A French naval surgeon and a fellow naval officer marched out of the prison at the rear of a column of sentries who had just been relieved from duty and were on their way back to the barracks. The light at this time of day would have been poor, creating ample opportunity for confusion with all the movement of sentries and prisoners, and the sentries would be keen to get back to the barracks after a hard day's work.

On 9 October 1809 a turnkey inadvertently left a war prison unlocked and a party of French prisoners took full advantage, spilling out into the yards. The sentry saw them and fired a shot at them, the ensuing commotion bringing Captain Cotgrave to the scene with 50 armed troops. Spotting a man on the wall, they fired and hit him. It turned out that he was one of the prison staff.

In February 1811 three privates from the Nottingham militia named Keeling, Smith and Marshal were heavily bribed to assist two French officers to escape. But a fourth soldier in the group who considered he was being unfairly treated by his colleagues informed the guards on duty. A military piquet was waiting on the other side of the wall. Private Keeling had given the French officers a pistol to use against local people who might challenge them but the prisoners turned it on the guards in a bid to evade capture. Luckily nobody was hurt.

On 28 February 1811 the three soldiers were tried and found guilty by court martial at Frankfort Barracks, Plymouth. All three were sentenced to be flogged and were awarded 900 lashes each, tantamount to a death sentence. Smith and Marshal were later pardoned (possibly by turning king's evidence) but Private Keeling, who had provided the pistol, received a reduced sentence of 450 lashes. These were to be carried out in the presence of piquets from every regiment in the garrison. Using a cat-o'-nine-tails meant 450 multiplied by nine cuts to the back, more than 4000 cuts to the bone. It was a brutal sentence in the extreme.

Thus, justice was served, and more importantly, seen to be done. The severe punishment and its marks on Private Keeling's back would be conveyed by the piquets to every regiment and unit in the garrison as a warning to those tempted to assist in an escape.

In March 1812 a civilian member of staff called Edward Palmer was found guilty of providing a disguise to a French prisoner named Bellaird. He was fined £5 and sentenced to six months' imprisonment. Such a sentence was all the more severe as his family would be evicted from the prison quarters immediately, with no money or food available to them.

In 1812 a man called Lynch who served on guard duties with the Roscommon militia attempted to assist three prisoners to escape. They paid him with counterfeit notes which they had made themselves and, on 12 March, when he tried to pass the notes he was arrested. He was sentenced at the Devon assizes for forgery as well as for helping prisoners to escape.

On another occasion a French prisoner was helping to build houses for staff outside the prison, the only houses completed at this time being those on Church Row. During the day he allowed himself to be built into a granite wall. When darkness fell he pushed over the wet masonry and made good his escape. No records exist to say whether he was recaptured or otherwise. Possibly, he made it to the coast and caught a lift across the Channel on one of the thousands of fishing vessels.

To aid them in their escape attempts some prisoners purchased English uniforms quite legally in the prison marketplace from the Jewish traders, just as Vanhille himself obtained clothing from his friend John Rowe.

Left: *A superb model guillotine carved from bone by a French prisoner of war. Models such as this and the frigate (inset), were sold in the prison market-place in order to raise money for additional food and clothes.*

Coin found in the marketplace during excavations by contractors in the 1980s.

Goods made in the prison to be traded for clothing and food included magnificent ships of the line made from bones with human hair for the rigging. The ships were superbly made, exact in every detail, by men who served on such vessels for many years. Examples are now held in many local museums, including the Burton Art Gallery in Bideford (a number of French prisoners of war were held in Bideford, in the area now known as Bideford Victoria Park, and when the town's gasworks were being constructed the graves of many of them were unearthed). Much prized by collectors, bone carvings have found their way into private hands, among them the model of the *San Pareil*, now owned by a Devonshire man. The *San Pareil* was a prison hulk off Plymouth from approximately 1810 until she was broken up in 1842. It appears that the French prisoner who made it was held aboard the *San Pareil* before being marched up to Dartmoor.

At last in 1814, with Napoleon apparently subdued and exiled to Elba after the Battle of Leipzig, large numbers of French prisoners were released. Interestingly, some chose to stay and married and raised families locally. Peace was not to last long. In March 1815 Napoleon left Elba with a thousand men, signalling the start of the 'Hundred Days' and a renewed outbreak of hostilities between the French and English, until his defeat on 18 June at Waterloo. Once again French prisoners started arriving back at Dartmoor; during the first four days of July, approximately 4000 were marched up from Plymouth, despite hostilities having ceased. Some were the very same men released just a few months earlier.

The last of their number did not leave Dartmoor Depot until February 1816, seven years after holding the dubious privilege of being the depot's first inmates. There was no longer the clank of steel rifle butts on the granite pavings and no longer the shouted orders. The animated chatter of the 9000 French prisoners which had hung in the air from 1809 until 1816 was gone. The prison became quiet and still as grass grew amongst the granite, and in the streets of Princetown the only sounds were those made by the birds.

Opposite, top: *A modern painting depicting the prison marketplace, looking up to main gate.*

Opposite, below: *Marketplace, looking down from main gate.*

Model ship, carved from bone by a
French prisoner at the Dartmoor Depot,
of the Napoleonic warship San Pareil.

Chapter Five
AMERICANS AND THE WAR OF 1812

It is sometimes difficult to know where English history ends and American history begins as far as North America is concerned. In the seventeenth century large numbers of British people (about 20 000 English left for New England alone), along with those from many other countries, set sail for the New World. Some went to escape oppression and others purely because they were swept up in the pioneer spirit.

These newcomers built up the country from the wilderness. They fought the Native Americans, taking their land to build new settlements which had little in the way of civilised comforts. It was often hundreds of miles from one town to the next and there were no established roads, no communication system and no postal service. But gradually these things were put in place, along with a democratic form of government.

As the country developed so the pioneers formed a more unified identity. Eventually it was inevitable that they should also want to govern their own affairs, rather than be ruled by a king thousands of miles away. This was the principal factor behind the American War of Independence (1775–76) which, after a bloody struggle against the British, saw the foundation of modern United States. Thus the War of Independence can be seen as the point at which American history became distinct from British history. But it was to be a later and rather more obscure war with Britain that found American prisoners being brought to Dartmoor, amid great confusion as to why the war had happened at all, and with many unsure to whom they owed allegiance, Britain or America.

It remains a common misconception that those Americans held as prisoners at Dartmoor were captured during the War of Independence. In fact it was the War of 1812, some thirty-five years later, that took them there. For many, particularly people in Britain, the events leading up to and during the War of 1812 are obscure. Some may have heard of the song 'The Battle of New Orleans', which describes the ignominious defeat of the British in Louisiana in 1815. This helped to avenge the fighting of a year earlier during which the White House was razed (later to be painted white to hide the smoke stains). The American national anthem, 'The Star Spangled Banner' is also said to date back to this war.

In the turmoil of those times, with so many on both sides having common roots, it is perhaps unsurprising that a number of the American sailors captured and held at Dartmoor Prison were English born. Having travelled to America to start a new life some had become sailors, signing on board American vessels only to find themselves captured by the English. Other American citizens, having been impressed into the Royal Navy or who had voluntarily engaged upon an English man-of-war, now found themselves under arrest having refused to fight against their fellow countrymen.

So why did the War of 1812 start? War was declared on Britain by the USA in response to Britain's impressment of sailors from US ships and its blockade of US ships during the Napoleonic Wars. A further factor was the desire of the

United States to put an end to harassment of American settlers in the North West (perceived to be an attempt by the British to colonise this territory), and to put an end to British influence over the Native Americans. The unseemly squabble over territorial issues was exacerbated by ideological factors such as a desire to uphold the prestige of the new-born republic.

In any event it was an unwelcome war and the Treaty of Ghent which signalled its end contained nothing to suggest that America had gained from fighting it, other than perhaps helping to forge unity and patriotism in the new nation. At least, as the protagonists, the Americans were spared having to make any major concessions to the British. Things had merely returned to the *status quo*.

Each side agreed to evacuate all enemy territory although the English were allowed to retain several islands between Maine and Nova Scotia. Any prize vessels taken beyond a certain date, ranging from twelve days off the American coast to one-hundred-and-twenty days in distant parts of the world, had to be returned to their owners. Each nation promised to make peace with the Native Americans and restore to the tribes all possessions, rights and privileges which they had enjoyed or been entitled to in 1811, before the hostilities began.

Each side also agreed not to carry off enemy property, and to return all prisoners of war as soon as possible. The treaty established commissions (three in all) to fix the boundary between Canada and America; also to establish the ownership of the islands between Maine and Nova Scotia known as the Passamaquoddy Islands. Both the British and the Americans agreed to endeavour to stamp out the slave trade. In retrospect this took quite a lot longer than promised, with the Civil War being necessary to end this trade in America.

The Treaty of Ghent was not binding on either party until ratifications could be exchanged. To this end, on 2 January 1815, Henry Carroll boarded the ship *Favourite* in London to take a copy of the treaty to the US, accompanied by Anthony Baker who carried a copy of the British instrument of ratification. The *Favourite* hit foul weather in the Chesapeake Bay and headed for New York harbour. Arriving at 8pm on 11 February 1815, news of her reaching port spread rapidly. A rider conveyed the news to Boston in a rapid thirty-two hours and shortly afterwards celebrations took place all over the United States.

During the War of 1812 a number of tremendous battles were fought. It is important to remember that the British were also engaged in the Napoleonic Wars, and the Peninsular War, with troops stationed in India, Australia and other areas of the world. Because of this the British could not raise the men and logistics necessary for the needs of their commanders in the America war. After three years of conflict, neither the US nor Britain could claim any great advantages. Militarily, it all ended in a bloody draw.

American prisoners taken during the conflict arrived in England to be sent to Plymouth where they were put aboard the hulks *Hector* and *Le Brave*. These two old battleships, deemed unfit for naval service, offered unsavoury accommodation for the miserable captives. The naval crew of the hulks comprised one lieutenant in command, one master's mate, one midshipman and 20 invalid seamen. The military guard on board comprised one lieutenant in command of guards, one ensign, one corporal and 35 soldiers. *Hector* and *Le Brave* were held at chain moorings about two miles from Plymouth Dock where resided Captain Edward Pellowe as officer commanding hulks and prisons ashore. As soon as prisoners were taken aboard the hulks, strict examinations of records were taken. The following information is from the general entry books, with the author's additions in brackets:

> *Current number* [given to prisoner by prison]
> *By what ship or how taken*
> *Time where* [date of capture]
> *Place where* [latitude and longitude often given]

In what ship [man-of-war, privateer, merchant]
Impressed, gave himself up, etc.
Prisoner's name [Christian name first]
Quality [rank]
Time received into custody [date]
From what ship or whence received
Place of nativity [place of birth]
Age
Stature [height]
Person [stout, thin, slender, heavy, medium]
Visage, face shape [round, oval, thin, long]
Complexion [sallow, pale, fair, fresh, yellow]
Hair
Eyes
Marks or wound scars [disabilities, missing eyes, tattoos, traumas, wounds, aesthetic items, freckles, moles, pierced ears, birthmarks]

Supplies of bedding and clothing were as follows:

Hammock
Bed
Palliasse [filled with straw]
Bolster
Blanket
Hat
Jacket
Waistcoat
Trousers
Shirt
Shoes
Stockings
Handkerchief
Exchanged or discharged signified by D. Died signified by DD. Escaped signified by E or R for ran.

The men were issued with their bedding and given the instructions, rules and restrictions to be observed. Every hulk had a physician attached to it who was, supposedly, always on board. On becoming sick the prisoner had to 'repair to' a separate part of the ship and be checked over by the physician. In reality doctors paid little attention to those who were ill. When death was deemed to be approaching, the prisoner would be taken to the hospital ship *Le Caton*. No more than one out of ten appear to have recovered.

Food for the prisoners on the hulks consisted of 1½ pounds of coarse bread, 8 ounces of beef including the bone, ⅓ ounce of salt, a quantity of barley and 1 or 2 turnips. This was issued on five days of the week and on the other two the men would have 1 pound of salt fish, 1 pound of potatoes and 1½ pounds of very coarse bread.

The American prisoners were described as troublesome and difficult to handle. The men were counted each night as they headed down below to bed. Every morning, very early, each prisoner was obliged to take his hammock on deck and leave it there for airing. He had permission to remain on deck or return below. No prisoner was permitted to hold correspondence, except by handing an unsealed letter to the Transport Board (as is the case with inmates today).

In order to prohibit liquor, newspapers, candles and other such items being brought on board, no boats were allowed to come alongside the hulks, a difficult brief for the guards because His Majesty's Dockyard was close by. Finally, on 2 April 1813 the Transport Board, fearful of escapes and their consequences, made an order to Captain Pellowe to remove all the prisoners in *Hector* and *Le Brave* to the Dartmoor Depot.

The prisoners were ordered on deck with their hammocks and baggage ready to march the 18 or so miles up to Dartmoor. A group of 250 men was selected and each was given a pair of shoes and his allowance of bread and fish for the day. Launches then took the men ashore where they landed at a place called New Passage. They were placed under a guard of soldiers equal in number to the prisoners and at 10.30am orders were given to march. The men were instructed to stay in line or risk instant death by shooting. Heavy rain fell during the arduous march to the war prisons. The men were allowed a little rest en route and when they arrived at Princetown snow was falling on to the frozen ground.

Three details taken from a modern painting of the Americans being marched up to the Dartmoor Depot, as visualised by the artist Prison Officer, Paul Deacon. The photograph below shows the moorland area along the route of their march today.

A full list of these first American men to occupy Dartmoor Prison is given in Appendix One. The men were all given a number as they were processed at the war prisons. They were the first of thousands of Americans to arrive at the prison and would begin an occupation that lasted until July 1815. The first American prisoner to be processed was a man called Michael Towers who was allotted prison number 1. Towers' birthplace was recorded as Hingham (there is a town called Hingham near Norwich in Norfolk), indicating that he was an Englishman. Certainly there were many English-born prisoners at Dartmoor. The list shows all 250 of these first occupants, the first being Towers and the last, prison No. 250, a George Gorling. The men were held as prisoners on the hulks as a unit and marched up to the prison as a unit, hence they suffered the fate of all prisoners – men known by numbers, rather than names.

The Americans marched into Princetown some time in the afternoon. One wonders what their thoughts were as they marched down Plymouth Hill towards the Plume of Feathers Inn and the Duchy Hotel, turned the corner at the Duchy and tramped the final half-mile to the prison gates at Dartmoor Depot. After 18 miles of rough ground, climbing to 1500 feet above sea level, they would have been tired, footsore, hungry and despondent. These men were fearful of the future and rightly so, as on arrival they were taken to the dreaded No. 4 war prison.

The prison was already hopelessly overcrowded with French prisoners. 'The Romans' were incarcerated in prison No. 4 and would certainly have been hostile towards the Americans. 'The Romans' called No. 4 'Les Capitole'.

The Americans, tired and bewildered, were dumped amongst mean, ruthless men in a festering building. Some of the newcomers were just twelve years old and must have been terrified. It is one thing to have the guards against you but when fellow prisoners are too, life becomes unbearable. Coming from the hulks very few of the Americans had any money or personal possessions, just a hammock and bedding that they each carried.

The view up Plymouth Hill, with the Duchy Hotel on the right. Although this photograph was taken eighty years or so after the American prisoners were marched into Princetown, this scene would have been much the same.

If one is to lay the blame for the treatment of these men on somebody then a portion of it must be laid at the door of the American Government. It took many months of applications to the American authorities before any action was taken to solve some of the prisoners' problems. It must have been doubly hard when many of the French prisoners in the same building had clothes, money, food and possessions in abundance. As weeks passed, more and more Americans arrived at Dartmoor, gradually filling prisons 1 to 7. As their number grew, so did the dissatisfaction of the Americans. They were unable even to buy soap or, perhaps more importantly, tobacco. With no means of improving their quality of life, it seems inevitable that an open revolt was looming.

Yet Captain Cotgrave decided that the best course of action would be to house all of the Americans in No. 4 prison, without moving 'The Romans', so that the overcrowding became even more severe. The Americans were locked up each night at dusk without light or heat. They fashioned small oil lamps from animal fat and cord and in No. 4 prison the scorch marks are still visible as the photographs of the cockloft illustrate (see page 44).

At daybreak they were marched into the open yard outside No. 4. Relations became very sour as even the sick prisoners were made to turn out of their hammocks. Brute force was the order of the day and the guards would thrust their bayonets into the hammocks and shout 'get out on parade' so that roll could be taken. As we have seen with the French, this involved about 1500 prisoners and took quite some time. Prisoners would collapse during roll which was taken regardless of rain, snow or the freezing fog, known as ammil by locals.

Initials carved on a beam by prisoners of war, in the period 1809 to 1816.

Prisoners were permitted to visit the other war prisons during the day but had to be sure to return to their own at dusk. The atmosphere between the Americans and 'The Romans' was simmering and one day a crowd of the latter lay in wait for the return of the Americans, armed with granite stones, clubs and knives. The Americans became trapped, cut off from their fellow prisoners and unable to escape, under ferocious attack until the guards were alerted by the commotion and regained control. At the end of the day some 40 men were taken to the hospital. No exact figures are available as such events tended to be hushed up.

Captain Cotgrave did inform the Transport Board of the event but put the blame on the American men. The Board were concerned by the actions of 'The Romans' and on 21 August 1813 the new agent for hulks and prisons received a communication from the Secretary Transport Board Admiralty as follows:

500 French prisoners are to be sent to the hulks and 500 men returned to Dartmoor from Mill Prison. These prisoners are being sent to the hulks because they keep selling their clothes etc and are to be put aboard prison hulks.

Walls were built on each side of No. 4 prison and the Americans were enclosed within the compound. On 16 October 1813 'The Romans' were forcibly scrubbed, clothed and marched to the Plymouth hulks where they remained until peace was declared. No. 4 was left to the Americans.

On 3 July 1813, 250 Americans were sent from *Hector* to the depot at Stapleton, in Bristol. They completed the march of 134 miles in eight days, guarded by 250 armed soldiers. These Americans were the lucky ones as Stapleton was far less crowded than Dartmoor. According to the general entry book, between December 1812 and April 1814, Stapleton held 421 prisoners while Dartmoor held between 6000 and 7000 Americans from April 1813 until July 1815.

On 4 July 1813 the prisoners managed to make and fly an American flag which they were ordered to remove but refused. Troops were sent in to remove it, with the upshot that they fired at the prisoners, wounding two.

On 29 May 1813 American prisoners made the following complaints known to their own agent, Reuben Beasly:

1. *The allowance is too scanty.*
2. *Whole day's allowance is scarcely enough for one meal.*
3. *The greater part of the prisoners are in a state of nakedness.*
4. *Some Americans enlisted out of the prison into Her Majesty's Royal Navy and were compelled to do it to better their conditions and preserve life in order to return to their own country. Make it known that unless something is done for our relief we must either enter service of our enemy or fall to famine and want.*
5. *There is a distinction between French and American prisoners, the French are allowed many privileges not permitted to the Americans.*
6. *The prisoner must hurry into the prison before dark, be locked up and remain without lights until 7–8am. If obliged to leave his hammock for any reason the prisoner might not find it again until light next day.*

Dr Dykar would not allow any American prisoner to be brought into the hospital until he was severely affected by illness and almost dead. Following his experiences in the War of Independence the doctor was of the opinion that every American was prone to skulking and shamming. Many also suffered as a result of Captain Cotgrave's ignorance.

The Dartmoor Prison general entry book is a valuable source of information regarding events at the prison. It informs us that the youngest American to be held as prisoner there was only ten years old. The youngest prisoner was a French boy of only nine years who was captured aboard a US vessel and taken to Dartmoor. These young boys were generally kept with their shipmates when captured which was the best thing for them. About 1000 Americans who were kept at Dartmoor were brought from Royal Navy ships of the line. They were experienced sailors who had refused to serve in British vessels against their own country. A small number, perhaps 60, did choose to serve in the navy rather than spend time at Dartmoor.

The Americans were extremely poor. Food was perhaps just adequate to prevent starvation but without money the men were unable to purchase additional food in the marketplace. In January 1814, as a result of repeated applications, Reuben Beasly received orders from the US Government to pay the prisoners an allowance. The first payment amounted to 1½d. per day which was later increased to 2½d. per day.

At around this time the US Navy sailors began to receive half-navy pay and some of the Americans who were ex-Royal Navy sailors also received their prize money earned while on board English men-of-war, despite now being on the 'enemy' side! With their new 'wealth' the Americans began to get involved in the market and conditions certainly improved.

The largest group of prisoners held comprised the men captured aboard privateers, approximately 2500, while the following figures show the numbers of prisoners taken from other vessels. From 'letters-of-marque' vessels (armed merchant ships authorised by a letter of marque giving permission from the US Government to engage in privateering), approximately 700 men. Approximately 1500 were taken from merchant vessels and 300 from non-US merchant vessels. There were about 500 US Navy sailors and approximately 50 marines and soldiers. The men serving on English men-of-war who gave themselves up rather than fight their own countrymen amounted to about 1000. The total of these figures is approximately 6550. The total of prisoners at Dartmoor was 6553 according to general entry books, although some of the entries are faint and water-stained and a few have not been completed by the prison clerks.

On 1 July 1815 a further 200 Americans were taken from the *Hector* and marched to Dartmoor where they were put into No. 4 war prison. Among these was a man called Charles Andrews who was second mate of the merchant vessel *Virginia Planter* which was caught off the coast of France by an English man-of-war, *Pyramus*. Andrews, who was thirty-six years old when captured, kept a diary while at Dartmoor which he called 'The Prisoner's Memoirs at Dartmoor Prison'. Though the journal contains several mistakes, one of which relates to the names of the dead who were killed on 6 April 1815 by the military (he states that a Captain Allen of the *Argus* died at Dartmoor though he actually died at Mill Prison in Plymouth), Andrews nevertheless gives us valuable insight.

A copy of a letter of marque, given to privateers by the US Government.

In Plymouth at the back of the Church of St Andrew is the Prysten Chapel in which there is a gravestone dedicated to Captain William Allen and midshipman Richard Delphy. In later years the stone was inscribed on the right-hand edge, 'repaired by the officers of the US ships *Susqehanna* and *Niagara*'.

So what is the connection here with the Americans at Dartmoor Prison? After the action the *Argus* crew were landed at Plymouth on 22 August 1813 and around 130 were subsequently held at Dartmoor Depot. The following members of the *Argus* are buried in the prison grounds:

James Henry, seaman, died 3 July 1814 after a fight with a fellow American, Thomas Hill. Henry born in New York.
Thomas Baron, servant, died 2 November 1813. Born in Norfolk, VA.
James Coombes, servant, died 20 March 1813. Born in New York.
Henry Addigo, soldier, died 23 December 1813. Born in New York.
John Montgomery, seaman, died 24 February 1814. From New York.
William Shaw, seaman, died 17 October 1814. Born Philadelphia.

The following is an extract of a letter describing the capture of the *Argus* sent from a Captain Maples to Vice Admiral Thornborough, addressed to John Wilson Crocker Esq., Secretary to the Commissioners of Admiralty 'His Majesty's Sloop *Pelican*, St David's Head, East Five Leagues, 18 August 1813'.

Sir,
I have the honour to inform you that in obedience to your orders to me of the 19 inst. to cruise in St George's Channel for the protection of the trade and to obtain information of an American sloop-of-war.
I had to board a brig, the master of which informed me that he had seen a vessel apparently a man-o'-war to the NE at 4 o'clock this morning, I saw a brig on fire and a brig standing by from her, which soon made out to be a cruiser.
I made all sail to chase and at half past five came alongside of her, she having shortened sail, and made herself clear for an obstinate resistance. When after offering three cheers our action commenced which we kept up with great spirits on both sides for 43 minutes.
We then lay her alongside and were in the act of boarding when she struck her colours. She proved to be the US sloop-of-war Argus *of 360 tons, 18 x 24-pounder cannonades, 2 long 12-pounders and had on board when she sailed from America two months since a complement of 149 men, but in the action 127 commanded by Lt Commander W.H. Allen who I regret to say was wounded early in the action and has since suffered amputation of his left leg.*
No eulogium I could use would do sufficient justice to the merits of my gallant officers and crew; which consisted of 116 men, the cool courage they displayed, the precision of their fire could only be equalled by their zeal to distinguish themselves.
But I must beg leave to call to your attention the conduct of my first Lt Thomas Welch, of Mr William Granville acting master, and Mr William Ingram, purser, who volunteered his services on deck and Mr Richard Scott, boatswain.
Our loss, I am happy to say, is small: the master's mate Mr William Young slain in his moment of victory while animating by his courage and example all around him, and one A.B. John Emery. Besides five seamen who are doing well, that of the enemy I have not yet been able to ascertain, but it is considerable.
Her officers say about 40 killed and wounded.
I have the honour to be
John Fordyce Maples
Commander.

PS. Captain Allen died of his wounds after he was landed at Plymouth and was interred with full military honours.

It is apparent that the Lords of the Admiralty were kept fully informed of all such matters. The funeral of the above Captain Allen was a spectacular event which all the Royal Naval captains of the port of Plymouth attended. This is a verbatim report of the proceedings from the time:

Plymouth, 24 August 1813
On Saturday last the 21st, was interred with military honours, William Henry Allen Esq. late commander of the United States sloop-of-war Argus, who lost his left leg in an action with His Majesty's sloop-of-war Pelican. J.F. Maples Esq. Captain, in St George Channel the 14th inst. Whereof he died in Mill Prison hospital on the 15th following.

Procession
Guard of Honour
Lt Colonel of Royal Marines with 2 companies of that corps
The Captains, Subalterns and Field adjutant
  (officers with hat bands and scarves)
Royal Marine Band
Vicar and curate of St Andrew's
Clerk of ditto
The hearse with the corpse of the deceased Captain Allen
  attended by eight seamen, late of the Argus,
    with crepe round their arms tied with white crepe ribbon
Also eight British captains of the Royal Navy as
  pall-bearers with hatband and scarf
Captain Allen's servants in mourning
The officers late of the Argus in uniform,
  with crepe sashes and hatbands, two and two
John Hawker Esq. late American
  Vice consul and his clerks
Capt. Pellowe, commissioner for prisoners of war
Dr McGrath, chief medical officer at Mill Prison Depot
Captains of the Royal Navy in port, two and two

This procession was followed by a numerous and respected retinue of inhabitants. The procession left Mill Prison at 12 o'clock. The coffin was covered with white velvet pall, on which was spread the American Ensign under which the action was fought. And upon that the hat and sword of the deceased were laid. On the coffin being removed to the hearse the procession moved forward with the band playing 'Dead March in Saul'.
On their arrival near the church the guard halted and clubbed arms single files inward through which the procession passed to the church. The corpse was carried in and placed in the centre aisle whilst the funeral service was read by the Revd vicar. After which the corpse was removed and interred in the south yard, passing through the guard in the same order from, as to, the church, on the right of Mr Delphy, midshipman of the Argus who lost both his legs in the same action and was buried the preceding evening, Friday 20 August 1813.

In the same paper, *The War*, the following appeared:

Plymouth, August 23
Arrived the Pelican brig and landed this morning the prisoners captured in the American brig Argus, these men were subsequently sent to Dartmoor as stated earlier but at first were held in the hulks at Plymouth.

The Transport Board wrote the following letter to Captain E. Hawkins on 26 August 1813:

Keep a vigilant lookout on the crew of the American sloop Argus which are now being delivered into your custody.

27 August 1813
Confidential memo from Rear Admiral G. Martin directs 'watch to be kept on American sloop Argus'.

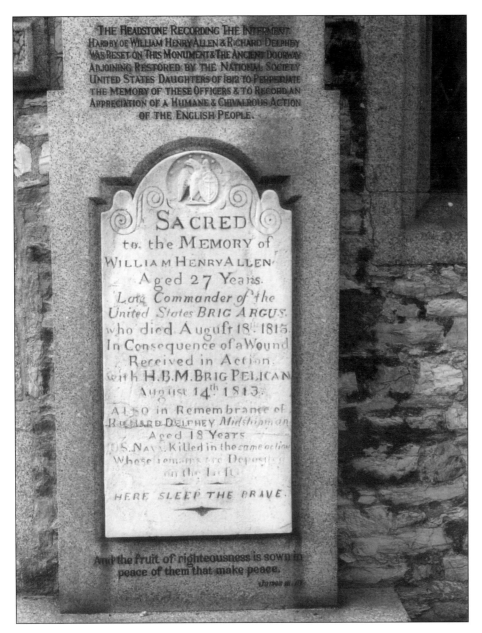

Above: *The step of The Door of Unity, at the rear of St Andrew's Church, Plymouth, along with a commemorative stone laid in 1930 by the United States Daughters of 1812.*
Left: *The gravestone of Captain Allen, in the Prysten Chapel of St Andrew's. The original headstone was incorporated in a new monument by the United States Daughters of 1812, in 1930.*

In the meantime, life at Dartmoor Depot was very difficult for the Americans. There were no possibilities of early release, no food, no decent medical attention and little protection from the cold weather. On 3 July 1814 two American prisoners Thomas Hill and James Henry, both former seamen from the *Argus*, exchanged heated words and later went to the cockloft to fight a duel. Henry was killed and Hill remained at Dartmoor. The Dartmoor general entry book contains the following note, '2109 Thomas Hill (*Argus*) received at Dartmoor Depot 3 August 1814 from Exeter Gaol, murder of James Henry'.

Charles Andrews, the American diarist, gives further information about the depot at this time. The book includes a certificate which has been signed by 62 prisoners, included a number of captains and senior-ranking members, which certifies that to the best of their knowledge the book was a true and accurate record of events. At least one member, Captain Charles Bennett, was a born-and-bred Englishman.

It is worth giving some insight into Andrews, as his historical record, despite its inaccuracies, is invaluable. He was a US seaman born in Newport, Rhode Island, and his number at the prison places him in the second batch of Americans to be held at Dartmoor.

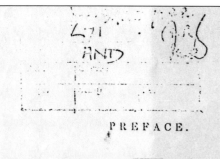

PREFACE.

The following pages are presented to the public by one of the survivors of this worst of prisons, believing it will be read with deep interest by every American, and by every relative and friend of those who happened to be one of the unfortunate inmates of the Dartmoor Prison.

If any part of the work should be found languid and tedious, it must be wholly attributed to the suffering situation of the author; the vigor and vivacity of whose mind was greatly affected by those of the body. If misery is less interesting collectively in groups than when viewed individually, let the reader single out one, and view him, separately, through the iron grating, and see him, pale and feeble, etching upon a stick, with a rusty nail, another notch, which adds to his calender another of those dismal days and nights he had spent in confinement; he may view him till he sees the iron enter his soul before he turns from him, and then say—it was my son, my brother, or my friend!—he will then have a picture interesting enough to his feelings.

COPYRIGHT SECURED.

CERTIFICATE.

We, the undersigned, late prisoners of war, having been confined the greater part of the last war between the United States of America and Great Britain, and having carefully perused and examined the following Manuscript Journal, kept by Charles Andrews, our fellow-prisoner at Dartmoor, in the County of Devon, in the kingdom of Great Britain, do solemnly declare, that all matter and occurences herein contained, are just and true, to the best of our knowledge and belief; and that this is the only Journal kept at Dartmoor.

Capt. Joshua Wait,	New-York.
Capt. Samuel H. Ginnodo,	Newport, R. I.
Capt. Frederick H. Coffin,	Hudson, N. Y.
Mr. Joseph C. Morgan,	Newport, R. I.
Lieut. Homer Hull,	—— Conn.
Mr. Jacob Evans,	Baltimore, Md.
Capt. Benjamin F. Chesebrough,	—— Conn.
Mr. Luther S. Dunbar,	Boston, Mass.
Capt. Richard Longly,	Portland, D. M.
Mr. Ephraim Abbott,	Boston, Mass.
Mr. Fenton Conner,	Charleston, S. C.
Mr. Joseph Conner,	Newbern, N. C.
Mr. David Morrison,	—— Pennsylvania.
Mr. Caleb Coffin,	Nantucket, Mass.
Mr. John Merrill,	Portland, Maine.
Capt. Charles Bennet,	Hudson, N. Y.
Mr. William Griffin,	Salem, Mass.
Mr. James Bowie,	do. do.
Mr. John F. Foster,	Gloucester, Mass.
Mr. Joseph Clark,	Cape-Elizabeth, do.
Mr. John Stafford,	Boston, Mass.
Mr. Charles Whitewood,	New-York.
Mr. Reuben Bunn,	do.
Mr. Samuel Rossett,	do.
Mr. Jacob F. Taylor,	Philadelphia.
Mr. William Conklin,	New-York.
Mr. Samuel S. Brush,	do.

Extract from Charles Andrews's book, showing the list of American prisoners who testified that his copy was a 'true copy of events and was the only journal kept at Dartmoor.' The prisoner highlighted was an Englishman by the name of Charles Bennett.

4	CERTIFICATE.	
Capt. John C Rowles,		Baltimore, Md.
Mr. John Meigh,		Boston, Mass.
Mr Edward Shaw,		Baltimore, Md.
Lieut. S. S. Fitch,		—— Connecticut.
Mr. Samuel Correy,		—— Vermont.
Mr. Samuel Howard,		Baltimore, Md.
Mr. William Clark,		Boston, Mass.
Mr. Joseph Fosdick,		do.
Mr. Samuel Morrison,		New-York.
Mr. William Hull,		do.
Mr. William Atkins,		—— Connecticut.
Mr. Daniel Hotchkins,		Salem, Mass.
Mr. Thomas Carlton,		Boston, do.
Mr. John Migat,		Warren, R. I.
Mr. Cornelius Hoy,		Baltimore, Md.
Capt. Jesse S. Smith,		Stonington, Conn.
Mr James Sproson,		New-York.
Mr. Benjamin Wheeler,		Baltimore, Md.
Mr. George Scott,		——, ——.
Capt. Matthew S. Steel,		Philadelphia, Penn.
Mr. W. P. Sevear,		Baltimore, Md.
Capt. James McQuilter,		do. do.
Mr. John S. Miller,		do. do.
Mr. Thomas Bailey,		Salem, Mass.
Mr. Warren Humphrey,		—— Connecticut.
Mr. William Rea,		Boston, Mass.
Capt. Thomas Hussey,		Hudson, N. Y.
Capt. James Boggs,		Philadelphia, Penn.
Capt. James Gays,		—— Virginia.
Capt. Thomas Mumford,		Newport, R. I.
Mr. Isaac Lowel,		Baltimore, Md.
Mr. Frederick G. Low,		Cape-Ann.
Mr. Henry Bull,		—— Connecticut.
Doct. Benjamin Mercer,		New-York.
Mr. Reuben Sherman,		—— Mass.

N. B.—Out of the above list there are, at this time, only nine survivors, as far as can be ascertained.

Andrews was five feet, seven inches tall and was of 'stout build', meaning he was muscular, with a long and sallow face, black hair, hazel eyes and with no visible scars. After his vessel the *Virginia Planter* was captured off Nantes by HMS *Pyramus* on 18 March 1813, Andrews was received at Dartmoor on 1 July 1813. On 3 August he was sent back to Mill Prison to be examined by a Mr Smith, returning to Dartmoor on 14 September 1813 and given a new prison number, 678. He was finally discharged on 20 April 1815 by the Board's Order, dated 16 March 1815, about four months after the Treaty of Ghent was signed.

On 29 July 1813 Captain Cotgrave gave orders that 120 American prisoners be transferred to Chatham. This would leave an excess of 500 at Dartmoor with plenty more held at the hulks in Plymouth. Discipline was strengthened and the Americans were not allowed out of No. 4 yard. At this time there was an outbreak of the dreaded disease smallpox and prisoners died daily. They were removed to the burial ground outside the prison.

The weather during that August was exceptionally bad. During the month there was only one clear day, which did not help tempers on both sides. The smallpox did not relinquish its grip until September 1813 but there was no respite for prisoners who survived as they were still short of food and allowances. Men were forced to steal from one another in order to live. A tribunal of American prisoners was organised to look into each theft and they would try prisoners who, if found guilty, would be sentenced to 24 lashes. Many were punished but they still had to survive on impossible rations. The agent for the Americans, Reuben Beasly, did very little to assist the situation.

One day during September 1813 Beasly visited Dartmoor at 3pm. The depot was cleaned prior to his visit and the guards prevented the prisoners from seeing him and protesting. This month also saw another draft of prisoners arriving from the hulk *Hector*. One of them, a man called Robinson, declared several of the crew of the *Argus* held at Dartmoor to be Englishmen. Seventeen of the prisoners were then taken to face trials for treason which were held on the *St Salvador*. If found guilty they would be executed at the yardarm.

The boatswain and a number of other crew of the *Argus*, wounded during the battle with the *Pelican*, had been taken to Mill Prison in Plymouth. In a bid to reduce the numbers at Dartmoor and to provide much needed crews for English ships, prisoners were encouraged to join the Royal Navy. As many were starving and had no money, quite a few took up the offer. They were then moved to the guardhouse out of reach of the other Americans who saw them as traitors. When a useful number of men thus recruited had been reached, they would be put on board a receiving ship and given a good bounty.

In December 1813 the cold was unbearable, making life torturous for the prisoners. But still they were forced to turn out each morning for roll call, some without shoes, stockings and jackets. They would cut up their only blanket in order to bind their feet against the cold and inevitable frostbite, but several died.

On 22 December 1813 there was at last a chink of good cheer when Captain Thomas G. Shortland RN took over from Captain Cotgrave and immediately promised to give more help to the prisoners. He ordered the doctor to visit them daily and remove any who were sick to the hospital. The winters on Dartmoor are always extreme but January 1814 was worse than usual. The leats froze solid leaving the prison without water and the foul leat for sewage could not be used. With each prison holding about 1500 men one can imagine the problems this caused. The stench must have been overpowering.

Snow was four feet deep on level ground, drifts would have been far deeper. The snow would blow up against the boundary wall and freeze hard, in effect creating a giant staircase right over the wall. In the 1970s when this happened there was no internal security-check fence and 600 convicts on exercise on the main yard posed a security nightmare. To remove snow from the wall earth-moving equipment was used but in 1814 there would have been no such means. It would be down to parties of prisoners to clear away the snow with shovels, with the first wind bringing it all back against the wall.

On 14 January 1814, eight American prisoners escaped over the wall, or rather walked over in blizzard conditions which on Dartmoor means a white-out where one cannot see beyond even a few feet. The author has experienced many blizzards on prison land and it is terrifying being unable to distinguish between land and sky, and life-threatening even when equipped with modern clothing. To a starving war prisoner it must have been purgatory. Seven were captured immediately and suffered even more when they were immediately put into the cachot on two-thirds rations.

The state of these men would have been terrible. With little food and no heat, their only bedding would have been a smattering of filthy straw between them and the cold granite. Imagine this for ten days in the worst winter in fifty years.

What of the one who got away? The lone prisoner wandered over the moor, completely and utterly lost and alone, until he came to the leat-man's hut out on the moors whereupon he was taken back to the prison. The poem contained in Charles Andrews's account perhaps best sums up this ill-fated escape attempt:

> On the 14th day of January
> The night ordained by fate
> For eight poor Yankee soldiers
> To try for their escape.
>
> Seven of them detected were
> And in the guard house lay
> The eighth resolved on liberty
> By chance he got away.
>
> The night being cold and dreary
> And he had far to go
> So this poor Yankee soldier
> Got hobbled in the snow.
>
> Discovered by his enemies
> That forced him back again
> Within the walls of Dartmoor
> Oppressed with cold and pain
>
> Shortland bred a seaman
> In Neptune's school was taught
> His heart compressed with pity
> Methinks I read his thought
>
> Saying go into the guard house
> And set those eight men free
> I'll show the sons of liberty
> There's honour still in me.

So it seems that Shortland took pity on the men and released them all from the cachot, putting them back into the war prisons with their compatriots. The prison roll at the time was upwards of 9000 French and American prisoners, with 1500 soldiers, officers and turnkeys. Prisoners were used to clear a pathway for the food wagons and, according to the records, all of the horses in the garrison, turnkeys, clerks and other available staff were thus employed. It must have been a testing time. At the end of January the weather began to improve and during February a thaw set in with the snow quickly melting. But further snow fell later; winter was not yet over.

On 5 February 1814 prisoners received 1½d. per day which meant that each prisoner received 4s. every thirty-two days. Things were getting progressively better. The prisoners at this time were not segregated into Black and White Americans (during the Second World War such segregation *was* practised between US troops stationed in the author's home-town in North Devon). But the Blacks were perceived to be troublesome in 1814. It is recorded that it was impossible to prevent them from stealing even though many were flogged. The Whites petitioned to have them removed and this was done. The Blacks were moved into No. 4 war prison where they more or less governed themselves.

During March 1814 the weather finally became milder and most of the snow disappeared. The American prisoners enjoyed the milder weather and were allowed into the marketplace to trade with merchants who came into the prison with produce. The market gates to the war prisons were often left open for the Americans to use.

The marketplace, looking up to main gate, c.1970s.

The marketplace from the opposite view, c.1970s.

A coffee shop was set up and coffee sold at 1d. per pint, though it has to be remembered that the allowance was just 1½d. per day. The prisoners bought goods at the market and some worked for the French in the production of straw hats. Many Americans managed to get clothing from the French and some of the young Americans worked as waiters. Men who had previously served in the Royal Navy received long overdue back pay.

In April 1814 a letter was received by Captain Shortland from the prisoners' agent, Reuben Beasly, saying that he was going to supply funds to Shortland to have coffee and sugar provided to the prisoners twice a week. He also confirmed that the 1½d. allowance was to be raised to roughly 2½d.

Contractors supplying goods for prisoners needed close control and supervision. At the end of March 1814 the contractors were found to be cheating on the weight of the rations, until Shortland intervened and put an end to the practice. In April another draft of prisoners was received from Plymouth. Conditions eased somewhat, the weather became warmer, and a school was set up for the young prisoners.

In May 1814 a new draft of 170 men marched from Plymouth to Dartmoor, arriving greatly distressed. They were cold, hungry and some were very ill. Among them were the 17 from the *Argus* who had been tried for treason. It appeared that there had been insufficient evidence to convict these English-born sailors who had fought for America. The court decided that they should be sent back to Dartmoor. The same month also saw cessation of hostilities with France and preparations were made to send the French prisoners home. Meanwhile, the Americans used their monthly allowance to buy furniture and other items from the French.

On 15 May 1814 Mr Williams, clerk to Agent Beasly, and a Jewish merchant from London, supplied and delivered to each of the prisoners a jacket, shirt, pair of trousers and shoes. The jacket and trousers were blue. Mr Williams states that all of the prisoners were to be clothed by the US from this point on and that each issue was to last for eighteen months. The men happily removed their yellow rags supplied by the Transport Board. In order to prevent American prisoners from selling their clothing they themselves passed an order that each man must wear his issued clothing when collecting his allowance. If this was not done then the allowance would not be given.

Orders for the first draft of Frenchmen to be released arrived on 20 May 1814. On the following day 500 were taken to the outer gate and marched to Plymouth where they were put on boats to France. Some had been many years at Dartmoor so one can imagine their joy and excitement en route to Plymouth. After a few days another draft of 1000 French was taken to the gate to make the same journey, with a number of French-speaking Americans released at the same time.

The Black (mullato and creole) prisoners who made up approximately 18 per cent of American prisoners (about 1150) were rowdy at this point and were confined to No. 4 war prison. The cockloft there was famous for its entertainment in the form of theatre, boxing matches and church services. It was a good gathering space for prisoners.

When released from the prison each man was expected to return all of his bedding, even if it had been issued many years earlier. If this could not be done then the release would not be permitted and it seems that the heartless depot staff could not give even a small amount of charity. A Frenchman who found himself in this terrible position after so many years of incarceration, could take no more and went back into the war prison and cut his throat. The incident was mentioned by an incredulous American prisoner, Perez Drinkwater, in his own letters home.

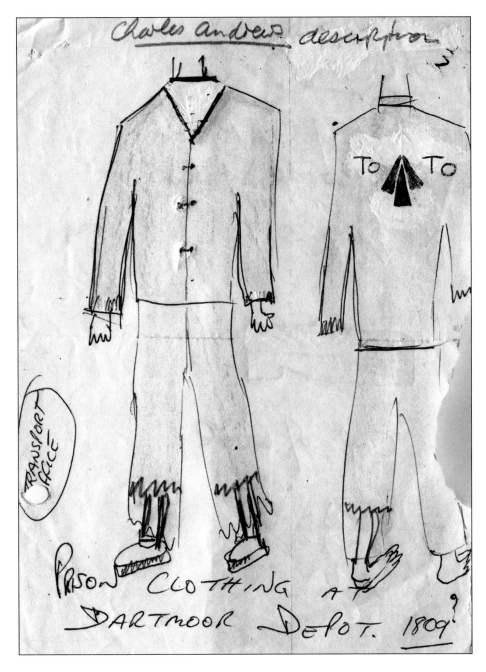

Description of the prisoners' yellow clothing, as recorded in Charles Andrews's book. The initials TO refer to the Transport Office (or Board), through which the clothing was supplied.

In June 1814 the weather was fine and Dartmoor seemed a more pleasant place than six months previously. The French were gone and it was announced that all remaining prisoners of war held throughout in the country should be sent to Dartmoor. This included prisoners from Chatham, Plymouth, Portsmouth, Reading and Stapleton.

By 20 June 1814 the only French left at Dartmoor were those in the hospital. A rumour circulated that the Americans would all be sent to Stapleton but this was quashed, and it was reiterated that all prisoners were to be concentrated at Dartmoor, including those currently held overseas.

In August a tunnel was excavated out of No. 5 war prison. But somebody talked and on 2 September Captain Shortland entered the prison with a strong guard. Tapping their crowbars against the lime-concrete floors until a hollow sound was heard, the tunnel was easily located. The prisoners were immediately removed from prisons 5, 6 and 7 whilst investigations were continued. The shaft was filled with large granite stones, each weighing more than half a ton. Charles Andrews states that the tunnels had been excavated to within 40 feet of the boundary wall.

It transpired that a prisoner called Bagley had walked up to a turnkey in the marketplace and had a brief talk with him. The prisoner was taken straight to the top gate, to Captain Shortland's house, and was never seen in the prison again. On checking the records the only Bagley that the author could find was a William Bagley, No. 6143 from the *Ajax*. Perhaps he was the informer, perhaps not.

On 2 October Beasly wrote to Shortland and informed him that a partial exchange was to take place shortly. Prisoners' spirits were lifted as nobody knew who might be exchanged. At this time a large Black prisoner called Richard Crafus was added to No. 4 prison. His number was 4603 and he was a giant of a man at 6ft 3¼in tall, heavily muscled and an expert boxer. He was captured aged twenty-two on the 'letter-of-marque' vessel *Requin*, taken to the Chatham hulks and was subsequently transferred to Dartmoor on 9 October via HMS *Leyden*.

Crafus was finally discharged around a year later on 15 June 1815 but during his time at Dartmoor he seized control of No. 4 war prison from the elected committee and ruled with an iron hand. He was a fearsome sight in his large hat and always carrying a massive club to inflict instant punishment on anyone whom he considered to be misbehaving. He was present on 6 April 1815 when the Dartmoor massacre took place, further details of which follow.

About 1000 Americans serving on board British men-of-war had given themselves up as prisoners of war rather than fight their own countrymen, and been dispersed to prisons and hulks. On 18 October 1814 orders were given by the Transport Office to discharge 62 men, formerly crew of the *Frolic*. They were taken to Dartmouth and put on a cartel by the name of *Jenny*. Unfortunately several members of the *Frolic* had not survived their stay on Dartmoor and are now buried on prison land. Among the dead were:

Prison number 2418 Darius Belloa RI [Rhode Island].
Prison number 2425 Daniel Appleton from Ipswich.
Prison number 2495 Edward Norton from Massachusetts.
Prison number 3595 Daniel Heny (alias Very) from Salem.

There were probably others who did not make it for the *Jenny's* trip back to their homeland.

The list of dead, supplied by the American cemetery at Cambridge, England, agrees with the above list but does not entirely tally with the general entry book list of prisoners who died at Dartmoor. But, as we shall see, the official list of 218 prisoners buried at Dartmoor does not include all American deaths, which amount to 271 (see Appendix One).

The winter of 1814–15 was extremely cold. Often prisoners visiting other war prisons would stay there after lock-up so that the roll for the individual war prisons the next morning was incorrect. After checking all the prisons, the figures would balance, but this prolonged the time prisoners stood on parade in icy weather suffering needlessly.

On 3 November 1814 the crew of the *Argus* were to be sent back to America. They were issued with a fresh set of clothing and taken to Dartmouth where they were put aboard the cartel *St Phillip* bound for the US. Confirmation of this was in the *Port News Plymouth* published on 18 November 1814 which stated that 'the cartel *St Phillip* was bound for America with American prisoners on board'.

On 17 January 1815 American prisoners were informed that Captain Shortland was to release them as soon as Agent Beasly was ready to receive them. At the same time, the last of the prisoners transferred from elsewhere, numbering 46, were being landed at Plymouth and taken to the Dartmoor Depot on 30 January 1815. This was about one month after the Treaty of Ghent had been signed and Britain and the USA were technically at peace.

Members present and the timescale of the Treaty of Ghent were as follows:

James Lord Gambier, Admiral of the Red Squadron.
Henry Goulburn MP, Under-secretary of State.
William Adams, Doctor of Civil Law.
The President has appointed the following:
James Quincy Adams
James A. Bayard
Henry Clay
Jonathan Russell
Albert Gallatin
(All citizens of the US).
All parties have agreed upon the eleven articles each going into detail on what is to be done to end the war and what territory is to be held by each party.
Treaty of Ghent concluded at Ghent 24 December 1814.
Ratification advised by senate 16 February 1815.
Ratification by President 17 February 1815.
Ratifications exchanged at Washington 17 February 1815.
Proclaimed 18 February 1815.

For the prisoners still awaiting news of their release there was mounting pressure and, tragically, some succumbed without ever knowing that freedom was imminent. One prisoner called John Butts Taylor from New York committed suicide by hanging in No. 5 prison, a tragedy recorded on 1 December 1814 by Charles Andrews. This is also confirmed in the general entry book which states that the man was only twenty-two years old.

It seemed that there was good news for Americans when the Treaty of Ghent was signed on Christmas Eve, 1814. The sloop-of-war the *Favourite* would sail with the treaty on 2 January 1815 and it was hoped that every prisoner would be released within three months. The spirits of the prisoners were now high and it was accepted that if the commitment was not carried through there would be trouble.

But the winter dragged on, with heavy snow on most days, and high spirits turned to restlessness and resentment which can only have been fuelled by the arrival, on 26 January, of a new draft of prisoners, despite the peace treaty. The officers amongst the prisoners were sent to Ashburton on parole. During February a great deal of snow fell and the temperature plummeted. Smallpox ran rife again and on 6 February distemper was also reported in the prison. A surgeon despatched to determine the cause reported that it was due to lack of ventilation. The cold weather continued throughout March.

On 4 March trouble erupted in the infirmary when George Johnson, an American prisoner of war, stabbed two nurses, one of whom was certainly a fellow American looking after sick prisoners. This man, Jonathan Paul, who died of his injuries, was from Charleston and had been impressed out of the *Hind* on 17 March 1813, taken to Chatham hulks and, along with Johnson, was sent to Dartmoor Depot, arriving on 3 August 1814.

Johnson, of the 6th American Regiment, was captured by British forces on 13 October 1812 in Canada and taken to Chatham hulks but did not arrive at Dartmoor until 31 October 1814. On 19 March, he was delivered to the civil authorities to be tried for the murder of Jonathan Paul. Presumably, although there are no records of the trial, he was executed, as there would have been many witnesses in the always overcrowded infirmary.

On the last day of March in 1815 the numbers at the prison were as follows:

No. 1 prison	*1769*
No. 2 prison	
No. 3 prison	*972*
No. 4 prison	*1051*
No. 5 prison	*958*
No. 6 prison	
No. 7 prison	*1263*
Employed in hospital	*19*
Employed in stores	*51*
Patients in hospital	*130*
Total held	*6213*

For some reason Nos 2 and 6, firm favourites for the prisoners to live in because they had wooden floors and slightly smaller areas, are listed as empty.

The ratified Treaty of Ghent was returned to England in mid-March, but still nothing happened to expedite prisoner release. The anger of the prisoners was hardly helped by the fact that the 2½d. allowance ended at this time because Reuben Beasly did not have the authority to pay it now that the war was officially over. An additional regiment of Somerset militia had arrived and a continuous stream of incidents heightened still further the bad feeling between guards and prisoners. Confrontations became common and the prisoners blamed Beasly for the lack of money. According to documents recently made available it is clear that the American and British Governments were at logger-heads over who was to pay for the ships to take prisoners back to the US.

The American Government thought that it was the responsibility of the British, saying that they would take all British prisoners to the British possessions of Halifax and Bermuda. Lord Castlereagh regarded this as an unfair distribution of costs as the British would have to ship to America *and* collect British prisoners from Bermuda and Halifax.

On 4 April 1815 Captain Shortland was in Plymouth and was concerned by the rising anger of the American prisoners. He went to the Citadel and asked that 200 soldiers be provided instantly to reinforce the Somerset and Derby militias at the prison. These 200 troops were provided under the command of Major Joliffe and he returned to Princetown with the troops. He found the prison peaceful but anger was still burning in the breasts of the Americans. All it needed was a small breeze to result in the fire becoming an inferno.

Chapter Six
MASSACRE
OR MUTINY?

On Thursday 6 April 1815, a little before 6pm, Captain Shortland was informed by his first clerk Mr Holsden that the prisoners were on a knife edge. He knew that trouble could erupt at any time and that a breach had been made in the wall that separated prison No. 7 from the barracks. Captain Shortland ordered the alarm bells to be rung and for troops to stand guard at the breach to prevent prisoners from climbing through. Weapons for the soldiers were stored near to the barracks and there was a possibility of these being seized by the prisoners.

The wall separating No. 7 war prison and the barracks, where the American prisoners made the breach which started the whole affair.

The drums beat out in the barracks, both internally and externally, calling the troops to arms and gathering staff together. The sudden commotion made the prisoners curious and they made their way outside to investigate, as they did so pushing against the gate leading to the marketplace. Apparently some of them had a bar and used it to break the lock on the gate. The officers were at their mess in the Duchy Hotel about half a mile away, having dinner.

Captain Shortland went at the head of the soldiers and ordered all of the men back into their respective prisons. They refused and, as the bread wagon was at this moment making a delivery to the stores, it was feared that the prisoners might attempt to take control. Again the order was given to return while the soldiers fixed bayonets and began to advance. Even when they were about three paces from the prisoners, the Americans stood firm and refused to back down. The order to charge was given and the prisoners instantly broke and ran as fast as possible to the safety of their prisons.

There were thousands of Americans desperately trying to get back into the buildings but they could not do so quickly enough. The order to fire was given. There is some doubt as to by whom but the Americans later insisted that it was Captain Shortland. The soldiers obeyed and fired a full volley, then several more, as prisoners fell dead and wounded all around.

DARTMOOR PRISON – A COMPLETE ILLUSTRATED HISTORY

An urgent message was sent to Admiral Sir J.T. Duckworth, C-in-C at Plymouth, who contacted Rear Admiral Sir Josiah Rowley Bart and Captain Schomberg, these two being the two most senior naval officers at Plymouth. They immediately went to Dartmoor Prison to inquire into the circumstances and report to Admiral Duckworth.

It was established that seven prisoners had been killed outright and seven were so severely wounded that amputation was necessary. Thirty-eight were dangerously wounded and 15 slightly wounded. The rudimentary medical care of those days meant that the risk of infection was great. Rowley and Schomberg presented the report stating that the rioters had endeavoured to overpower the guard and force open the prison. It was further stated that the rioters seized firearms and that five were killed and 34 wounded. The prisoners vehemently denied this and formed a committee to issue their own report.

The prisoners' report says that on 6 April 1815 at about 6pm all of the prisoners were quiet in their yards. It was about time to turn in for the night when the alarm bells were rung. Many prisoners ran into the square where they saw the troops lined up and at the same time a number of soldiers climbed on to the walls around the prisons. The order to return to prisons was given, followed by the order to fire. The prisoners ran back to the prisons to find only one door open. The troops on the wall then opened crossfire and the soldiers fired into the doors and windows of the war prisons.

The prisoners appointed a committee who presented this report, signed by each of the ten members of the committee, the next day. It accurately recorded the number of deaths, unlike Schomberg and Rowley's report.

On 8 April the coroner, Mr Joseph Whitford, held an inquest at the prison where it was established that seven men had been killed: John Haywood, James Campbell, Jesse Severedge, Joseph Took Johnson, Thomas Jack, John Washiil and James Mann.

The coroner's jury, composed mainly of Dartmoor farmers, issued a verdict of justifiable homicide. Unfortunately the coroner misspelled three of the names, the flowing ink pens of the clerks presenting a few problems. For example, Jesse Severedge was actually William Loveredge, John Washiil was John Washington and Thomas Jack was Thomas Jackson. There were 34 prisoners with the name of Jackson, only one of whom died at Dartmoor, almost a year previously. Thomas Jackson died on 7 April 1815 and was just fourteen years old. The correct list of names, preceded by the prisoner's number, reads:

3134	John Heywood	Maryland	Aged 25
2647	James Campbell	New York	Aged 36
4884	Wm Jesse Loveredge	New York	Aged 18
1347	Josh Tooke Johnson	Connecticut	Aged 19
970	Jabez Mann	Boston	Aged 30
6520	Thomas Jackson	New York	Aged 14
3936	John Washington	Savannah	Aged 25

The American representatives demanded a further investigation so an Englishman named Mr Larpent and an American called Mr Charles King were appointed to investigate fully. They did so and on 26 April 1815 presented their report to Mr Adams, the Minister of the United States to the British courts. It was a whitewash, drawn up so as not to offend the newly declared peace that had been signed in December. It was recognised that the British and the Americans now worked together, as they did for the report, in an effort to get the American prisoners back home.

The American minister asked that Captain Shortland might be placed on trial but did not press it as American witnesses would have to travel back to England again for any subsequent trial. English newspapers likewise made little of the incident; both countries seemed fed up with the unnecessary war from which nobody had benefited.

Before the prisoners left Princetown they held a mock trial of Reuben Beasly and found him guilty of taking no interest in the departing US prisoners, then they hanged him in effigy. On 19 April 1815 the prisoners made the long march to Plymouth with bare feet and poor clothing, walking away from Dartmoor, never to return.

Captain Shortland was blamed for the massacre of prisoners by the Americans as various witnesses swore he gave the order to fire. The British Government attached no blame to Captain Shortland who was promoted to superintendent of Port Royal Dockyard in Jamaica where he died from yellow fever in 1825. The controversy rumbled on over the years and in 1906 William Crossing in his *Western Morning News* story 'Princetown: Its rise and progress' referred to Captain Shortland and the Princetown Massacre in 1815. This prompted a stern reply in the paper on 2 April 1906 from the grandson of Shortland, Commander Fred Shortland:

Sir,
In yesterday's Western Morning News *in an article 'Princetown: Its Rise and Progress' an offensive attack is made on the honour and courage of my grandfather Captain T.G. Shortland RN, Governor of Dartmoor Prison, in 1815, taken from an account written by Charles Andrews, one of the captives and printed in a New York paper in 1852, or thirty-eight years after the event.*
Captain Shortland was promoted from Lieutenant to Commander for gallant conduct in cutting out the French brig L'Avanturier *from the Bay of Corrigeon in 1798, being at that time First Lieutenant of* Melphomene, *Captain Sir C. Hamilton, and commanding the boats of that ship and* Childers *sloop on this expedition.*
He reluctantly gave the order to fire on the prisoners who had revolted, and when there was grave danger of the guard being overpowered, and by this act saving further bloodshed.
He was tried for this at Exeter and acquitted of all blame, and remained as governor for some time after, and was thought so well of by the Admiralty that he subsequently held some of the best appointments open at that time to Post Captains.
He died of yellow fever some ten or twelve years later at Jamaica when captain of Magnificent *and Commissioner of Port Royal Dockyard. I don't see what good Mr Crossing serves in taking away the good name of a gallant gentleman, who died doing his duty eighty years ago, and causing needless pain to his descendants.*
He must remember that in 1852 the feeling between all people of this country and the United States was not of the same cordial nature which it happily is at this time.
This account can be supported, I have no doubt by Mr Crossing from papers at the Admiralty.
Fred Shortland, Commander Royal Navy (Retired).
Ash Cross House, Stoke Gabriel, South Devon.

The letter from William Crossing in reply was written on 2 April 1906:

Sir,
Referring to the letter on this subject in your issue of today, I very much regret that my reference to the disturbance at Dartmoor Prison of the War of 1815 should have given pain to the descendants of the Governor Captain Shortland.
I was of course actuated by no other motive than to give what I believed to be an accurate account of the event, and as I stated in my article, I derived my information from a pamphlet by Charles Andrews, who was a prisoner at Dartmoor.
He kept a journal while there, and the pamphlet is the result of that. His statements are attested by a number of his fellow prisoners who solemnly declare that all matters and occurrences herein contained are just a true to the best of our knowledge, and belief, and that this is the only journal kept at Dartmoor.
But this pamphlet was not my sole authority, much of my information I

gleaned more than forty years ago from people who well remembered the days of the war prisons.

I am not contending that my information from either of these sources is correct, I am only stating whence I derived it. An account of the Dartmoor War Prison, however brief, could not well be written without some mention of this regrettable affair, but I can assure your correspondent that had I thought my remarks would be likely to give pain, I should even at the risk of being considered an imperfect chronicler, have made only the barest reference to the matter.

William Crossing, 2 April 1906.

The above letter goes to show that not too much emphasis can be placed on Charles Andrews's account, even though many prisoners signed his certificate stating it to be true.

THE DRINKWATER LETTERS

The author established contact with an American lady, Kimberley Vanderveer, a direct descendant of another prisoner, Perez Drinkwater, whose notebooks and letters home to his brother Eldredge contain fascinating details about the massacre/mutiny and his time at Dartmoor.

Mrs Vanderveer confirmed her relative served as a lieutenant on the 'letter-of-marque' vessel the *Lucy*. Bruce Felknor's web page on the subject also confirms that Perez Drinkwater was a lieutenant aboard the privateer schooner *Lucy* when he was captured by HM brig *Billerkin* during the last days of 1813.

There is some mystery here as to whether Drinkwater was transferred to the 'letter-of-marque' *Siro* a little while later. According to the Dartmoor general entry books he was a crew member of the *Siro* when it was captured at sea on 13 January 1814. The author's records of American prisoners at Dartmoor show only two called Drinkwater, Perez and another called Daniel, and no prisoners as having served on the *Lucy*. Here is Drinkwater's entry:

Prison number	937
By what ship or how taken	Pelican
Time when	13 Jan 1813
Place where	At sea
Name of prize	Siro
Man-o'-war, privateer or merchant vessel	Letter of Marque
Prisoner's name	Perez Drinkwater
Quality [rank]	3rd Lieutenant
Time when received in custody	31 Jan 1814
From what ship received or how received	Plymouth [hulks]
Place of nativity [where born]	Port...[indistinct]
Age	25
Stature [height]	5ft 9ins
Person	Stout [means muscular]
Visage and complexion	Long haired [beard?]
Hair	Brown
Eyes	Hazel
Marks or wounds	None
Date of supply [clothes, bedding etc]	20 Feb 1814
Exchanged, discharged died or escaped	Discharged
Time when	10 April 1815
whether, and by what order discharged	Boards Order 7 April 1815

It is possible to check on the accuracy of his letters home. He states in his letter to his brother, dated 20 May 1814, that he landed on the Plymouth hulk *Brave* on 24 January 1814, and was marched up to the depot at Dartmoor on 31 January 1814. This date agrees with prison records.

In his letter to his parents, dated 8 April 1815, just two days after the massacre, Drinkwater states seven were killed, 38 dangerously wounded and 30 slightly wounded, which again is correct. He added that he would be leaving on 9 April 1815 for London (this would be to meet a cartel ship). Perez Drinkwater of the *Siro* was discharged on 10 April 1815 (perhaps there was a small administrative delay) so again, correct. Further, he added that one of the crew of the *Siro* was killed in the massacre – 970 Jabez Mann, aged thirty, from Boston, was certainly killed on 6 April 1815 – and that John Strout of the *Siro*, belonging to Portland, died. 951 John Strout, aged sixteen, of Portland, died on 20 January 1815. He names two others of the *Siro* who died as prisoners: 946 John Perkins, aged twenty-five, from Newhampton (died 3 Nov. 1814), and 953 William Thompson, aged twenty-five, from Port Prince (died 18 April 1815).

So it seems that everything Drinkwater has said in his letters home is correct and that he was a most accurate and well-informed man.

Bruce Felknor, in his comments on the letters home, says, 'Perez Drinkwater did eventually return home, and took up post-war life and activity in community affairs, and died an old man full of age and honours.'

Kimberley Vanderveer told the author that Drinkwater left a notebook, written mainly aboard the *Lucy*, but the last few pages in Dartmoor, with a layout of the prison. Most of the notebook was very technical, including sailing and navigational problems and possible solutions, trigonometrical theorems and the like; the work of an exacting and precise man.

Here are some of his letters home:

A.D. 1815 DARTMOOR PRISON Ap. 8th

Honored Parents

I have the pleasure to inform you that I am in good helth and my best wishes are that when these few lines Come to hand they may find you the same and all my frinds. Dowtless you have heird of the marcichre [massacre] of Dartmoor in which ther was 7 killed and 38 wounded, it was done on the 6th of this month, the soldiers fired on us when we were all in the yard about 5000 they fired on us in all directions and after we was [back] in the prison they killed a number in the prison. It was one of the most retched things that ever took place Amonghts the savages much more amonghts peple that are the bullworks of our religion. I had the good fortin [fortune] to escape their fury, but they killed some while begging for mercy after being wounded they likewise kicked and mangle the dead right before our faces. Pain Perry of North Yarmouth was one that was wounded but not bad....
I shall leave heir to morrow morning for London and from their to Crownstad and from their to Portland in the brig Albert *of Portland I think it will be much more to my advantage than to return home in a corveat [corvette] as it will be some time before it comes to my turn... There is a number of men here that belong to Yarmouth, Falmouth, Freeport and Pownal that will inform you of the Late mascree [massacre] at this place... one of our Crew was killed in the Late Marseehree [massacre] his name was James Man two has died besid John Strout belonging to Portland tomorrow will be a happy day if I live to see it as I shall get my liberty Please to remember me to my friends & to my Wife I hope that you [will] assist her till my return which I hope will be in 4 months.*

I remain your obedient son,

PEREZ DRINKWATER

Dartmoor Prison Saturday Morning, May 20th, 1814

Dr Brother

… We arrived into Plymouth on the 20th of January was put on board the [prison-ship] Brave on the 24th and was landed from her on the 31 and marched to this place in a snow storm. This Prison is situated on one of the highest places in England and it either snows or rains the whole year round and is cold enough to wear a great coat the whole time there is 10,000 of us here now but the French are about going home…
This is the first time that I was ever deprived of my Liberty and when I sit and think of it it almost deprives me of my sences for we have nothing else to do but sit and reflect on our preasant situation which is bad anough god noes for we have but 1 lb and a half of black bread and about 3 ounces of beef and a Little beef tee to drink and all that makes us one meal a Day the rest of the time we have to fast which is hard times for the days are very Long heir now I want to get out of heir before the war is over so that I can have the pleasure of killing one Englishman and drinking his blood which I think I could do with a good will for I think them the worst of all the human race for their is no crimes but what they are gilty of…
… yisterday they called up 500 French men to go away their was one that had been in prison Nine years and had worn his blanket out so that he had but half of it to give those rebels and on that acount they sent him back and put him on the bottom of the books for exchangeing, the man took it so hard that he cut his throught and was found dead between the prison dores, and a thousand other such deeds they have, been guilty of since we have been conmed heir in this cursed place and a monght these rebels for I can call them nothing better and I shall never dye happy till I have had the pleasure of killing one of them which I am determined to do if an oppenity ever offers to me to doe it…
… we have plenty of creepers [insects such as bedbugs and lice] heir to turn us out in the morning, them and the Englishmen together don't Let us have much peace Day nor night for they are both enimyes to us and Likewise to peace and the more they can torment the human rase the better they are pleased…

I hope that you will write to me every oppertunity that afford you to do for it would be a happy thing for me to heir from you I have wrote several Letters to you be fore and shall still continue to write every oppertunity, you must tell Sally to bare her misfortunes with as much fortitude as she can till my return I must conclude with wishing you all well. So god bless you all and be with you for I cannot.

From your sincere friend & Brother

PEREZ DRINKWATER

Royal Prison, Dartmore Oct. 12th 1814

Dear Sally

It is with regret that i have to inform you of my unhappy situation that is, confined heir in a loathsom prison where I have wourn out almost 9 months of my days; and god knows how long it will be before I shall get my liberty again… I cheer my drooping spirits by thinking of the happy Day when we shall have the pleasure of seeing you and my friends…
The same place is one of the most retched in this habbited world… neither wind nor water tight, it is situated on the top of a high hill and is so high that it either rains or hails or snows almost the year round for further partickulars of my preasant unhappy situation, of my strong house, and my creeping friends which are without number…
… my best wishes are that when these fe lines come to you they will find you, the little Girl [his daughter] my parents Brothers sisters all in good helth I have wrote you a number of letters since my imprisenment here and I shall still trouble you

with them every oppertunity that afford me still I have pleasure of receiving one from you which I hope will be soon...

I am compeled to smugle this out of prison for they will not allow us to write to our friends if they can help it... So I must conclude with telling you that I am not alone for there is almost 5000 of us heir, and creepers a 1000 to one...

Give my Brothers my advice that is to beware of coming to this retched place for no tonge can tell what the sufferings are heir till they have a trial of it. So I must conclude with wishing you all well so God bless you all. This is from your even [ever] derr and beloved Husband.

Chapter Seven
MARBLEHEAD

Top: *A painting of Captain William Stacey of Marblehead who was just seventeen when he was first sent to the Dartmoor Depot.*
Above: *A photograph of Stacey on his return to Marblehead. He continued his career at sea and became a famous sea captain, ending his days as Inspector of the Customs House in Marblehead.*

I wanted to choose a small American town as representing the places from which men were sent to fight in the War of 1812. Marblehead chose itself.

During my research into the American involvement in Dartmoor Prison I came across several mentions of a town called Marblehead in Massachusetts. At one time there were 500 Marbleheaders held at Dartmoor Prison, and as well as being involved at the forefront of the War of 1812, they also figured significantly in the War of Independence. This was intriguing.

As a principal officer at the prison, I was responsible for organising the archive records into some sort of system. I went to the roof space in which the old records were housed and began to sort them out with the intention of compiling an index of sorts. One file was marked miscellaneous and as I took it out I saw the pale blue corner of an airmail letter. It was from the United States and the sender's address was Marblehead; that place again!

The letter was from Marjorie Mace of Marblehead who was asking the governor of the prison whether she could visit. Her great-great grandfather, William Stacey, had been held as a prisoner of war at Dartmoor. As a young seaman aboard the US privateer *Alfred* he had been captured and taken to the hulks in Plymouth from where he was sent to Dartmoor Prison. Her great-great-great uncle, Stephen Stacey, had lost his life at Dartmoor Prison and lies buried there.

Fascinated by the letter which had been sent a few years earlier, and wondering whether Mrs Mace was still alive and at the same address, I wrote to her. Her prompt reply was thrilling as it last provided a direct link to the War of 1812.

As prison historian part of my duty was to escort historical groups around the prison though I was not allowed to escort ordinary members of the public. On seeing the governor I asked him if I could invite Mrs Mace inside the prison to see the areas in which her ancestors had been held. He readily agreed and Mrs Mace then informed me that she would be one of a group of 38 Marbleheaders travelling to the UK to visit their twin town of Fowey in Cornwall.

On the morning of the visit I received a call from the gatekeeper as the visitors arrived, and walked to the gate to greet them. With a definite air of excitement we set off down through the marketplace where so many prisoners of war had made and sold their beautiful goods or exchanged them for food and clothes.

Finally, with Mrs Mace at the head of the column, I took the party to No. 4 prison's cockloft, the same one in which I had discovered scorch marks on the beams and hammock hooks wrapped in the cloth from war prisoners' clothes. It felt like a time capsule when I discovered it; the visitors, too, were enthralled and spoke in whispers. This is a part of the prison rarely seen by anyone at the prison and it exudes a powerful presence.

Mrs Marjorie Mace, (top left and right) in No. 4 war prison roof where her great-great grandfather William Stacey was held during the War of 1812, and (above and left) in the American cemetery where her relative Stephen Stacey is buried.

The subdued visitors had seen all that they wanted to. I made no attempt to hurry them as the experience was so special. Those who had ancestors who were held at Dartmoor talked of the place long into the night. Later I received two invitations, in 1992 and 1995, to visit Marblehead which I eagerly accepted. During these visits I was able to discover a lot of the spirit of the place and also found the Marbleheaders themselves to be my kind of people. They were straightforward, honest, would not back away from confrontation and, I feel, even today would be magnificent people to have in the trenches with you.

I had for the moment satisfied myself with the history of the American prisoners of war at Dartmoor but was now curious about English prisoners of war held in America. At Marblehead there is Fort Sewell which in the War of 1812 was used to hold the British. In a book called *The History and Traditions of Marblehead*, written by Samuel Roads Junior and published in Marblehead in 1897, I found on page 314:

> *During the month of February 1814 a number of British prisoners were brought to Marblehead and confined in Fort Sewell. This action on the part of the government was seriously resented by some citizens many of which declared that if the opportunity offered they would inflict summary vengeance on the English, in retaliation for the inhuman treatment of American, but mainly Marblehead prisoners, by the British. Finally as a measure of caution the prisoners were removed and carted off to Boston and held there.*

The town records Vol. 5 – 10 March 1810 to June 1837 states:

> *A meeting be convened to discuss that British prisoners of war now confined as hostages in the US be removed from thence to this town and to be confined in the Fort here, and that accommodation be provided to cater for their accommodation. This meeting is called to get the opinion of the inhabitants.*
> *Signed Joseph Barker, Benj Knight, J. Sparhawk. Select men of Marblehead.*

Fort Sewell in Marblehead where British prisoners of war were held during the War of 1812.

Internal view of Fort Sewell, prisoners' accommodation.

The inhabitants agreed to send the prisoners to Fort Sewell but after a short time the decision was altered and, as mentioned before, the men were sent to Boston in the interest of their safety. Fort Sewell is a dark, dank dungeon, a terrible place. Yet, as with Dartmoor, there are interesting records of its role.

The fort has a chequered history. During the War of 1812 the fort's gunners protected the US frigate *Constitution* when she sailed into Marblehead to prevent capture by the English frigates HMS *Tenedos* and HMS *Endymion*. A Marbleheader on board the *Constitution* guided her through the rocks which lay just below the surface; the British frigates, of course dared not follow.

The Essex Institute Historical Collections, page 252, states:

> *Jonathan Williams, a grand-nephew and former business associate of Benjamin Franklin, was appointed Mayor and Inspector of Fortifications. In 1801 he described Fort Sewell at Marblehead as an irregular oblong figure with a block house, one side of which was above a wall and arch, forming a magazine below.*

The Fort at Marblehead was positioned at the upper end of the Revolutionary War Fort (1775). Another 275 feet of the wall of the old battery was left to serve as a covered communication from the town to the fort, three of the seven-foot outer walls of earth were supported by dry stones two feet thick on the inside. The rear wall bisected by the new block house was to be constructed of stones or bricks 18 inches thick and nine feet high. The Marblehead Fort mounted one 42-pounder, five 24 and 18-pounders on coast carriages, with the four, nine and six-pounders on travelling carriages.

The armament was considerable for such a small fort. The fort at Marblehead received considerable appropriations of $11 700 and underwent improvements from 1799 until 1801. The fort was enlarged and the magazine and barracks were built into the slope outside and beneath the 1794 fort. This was under the direction of Mayor Louis Tousand (1749–1817).

The fort was named in honour of a local Federalist congressman called Samuel Sewell (1757–1814) who had served several terms as the town's representative to the General Court, and served as a congressman from 1796 until his resignation in 1800. At this point he became a State Supreme Court Justice and eventually Chief Justice.

I could find little information about the British at Fort Sewell as there were no available records. But in all prisoner-of-war camps the incidence of deaths was high, owing to poor food, medical care and living standards. There were many other prisons holding English troops near Marblehead, such as Pittsfield and Salem on the North River; hulks were also used to house prisoners as in Plymouth. I did find the following information about Marblehead deaths, some of which are linked to Dartmoor Prison:

872   *William Fletcher, 12 October 1813, a prisoner in England, a prisoner at Dartmoor and was buried there, prison number 69.*
874   *A soldier, 25 October 1813, died of consumption at Fort Sewell, buried at Marblehead.*
900   *James Lovett, General Hampton's Brigade, 14 December 1813, killed at his post by an Indian.*
963   *William Follett, 29 March 1814, on board prison ships and buried there.*
980   *Charles Francis, 4 August 1814, shot by the sentry at the Fort and buried at Marblehead.* [Perhaps an English prisoner?]
996   *Amos Grundy, 14 September 1814, a prisoner in England and buried there.*
997   *Edward Brown, 15 September 1814, a prisoner in England and buried there.*
998   *William H. Ellinwood, 15 September 1814, a prisoner in England and buried there.*
999   *William Pousland, 14 September 1814, a prisoner in England and buried there.* [Note, he died on the Chatham Hulks, his Chatham No. 3240.]
1000 *Isaac S. Clough, 15 September 1814, a prisoner in England and buried there.*
1001 *Joseph Andrews, 15 September 1814, a prisoner in England and buried there.*
1002 *John Smith, 15 September 1814, a prisoner in England and buried there.*
1003 *William Hammond, 15 September 1814, a prisoner in England and buried there.*
1034 *Samuel Hammon, 5 January 1815, at Salem Fort, buried at Marblehead.*
1039 *Thomas Courtis Captain, 9 January 1815, a prisoner in England and buried there.*
1067 *John Adams Junior, May 1815, a prisoner in England and buried there.*
1072 *Josh Lackey, 2 June 1815, at Dartmoor Prison and buried there, prison number 4486.*
1073 *John Kelley, 2 June 1815, died of dropsy at Dartmoor Prison and buried there, his prison number 3756.*
1074 *Joseph Wedger, 2 June 1815, a prisoner in England and buried there.*
1075 *Thomas Jarvis, 2 June 1815, at Dartmoor Prison and buried there, prison number 5321*
1086 *Richard Lee, 7 August 1815, at Dartmoor Prison and buried there, prison number 6126.*
?   *Stephen Stacey, 12 April 1815, at Dartmoor Prison and buried there, prison number 5750.*

These details are from Marblehead Town Hall records held at the town's Abbot Hall and give some indication of the loss incurred by the town in the War of 1812. It seems that the information was recorded in batches on the day it arrived on incoming ships as it is unlikely that all those recorded as dying on 15 September 1814 did so on the same day. When compared with the record books at Dartmoor, the Marblehead dates are always two months later.

A Captain Glover Broughton, a prisoner from Marblehead, drew an extremely accurate plan of Dartmoor Prison, showing the massacre taking place and the soldiers firing at the retreating prisoners. He stated that 500 Marbleheaders were held there at the time and, as a mature man, he would have known all of the men from his home. The external barracks are not shown on his plan as, of course, he never saw them, but he would have been familiar with the internal barracks in the petty officers' prison over the wall from war prison No. 7. He also drew the water tower outside the main gate, which he would have passed on his way in and when leaving on discharge. It was a pleasure to have the present-day Glover Broughton sign the plan drawn by his great-great grandfather.

Glover Broughton's details taken from the general books at Dartmoor:

Prison number	764
By what ship, how taken	*Taken out of the* Pallas
Place where	[not given]
Name of prize	Pallas
Man-o'-war, privateer, merchant vessel	*Privateer*
Prisoner's name	*Glover Broughton*
Quality [rank]	*Seaman*
Time into custody [at Dartmoor]	*3 November 1813*
From whence received	*Plymouth*
Place of nativity [birth]	*Marblehead*
Age	*17*
Stature	*5ft 4ins*
Person	*Slender*
Visage, complexion	*Light*
Eyes	*Blue*
Marks or wounds	*None*
Date of supply [clothes, bedding]	*1 November 1813*
Exchanged, discharged, died or escaped	*Discharged 26 April 1815*
Boards Order	*16 March 1815*

Captain Glover Broughton's drawing of the massacre of 6 April 1815.

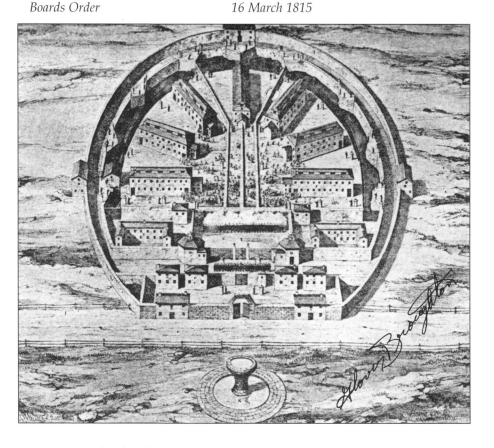

Glover Broughton's key to his drawing on page 90.

A KEY

TO THE VIEW OF DARTMOOR PRISON, ENGLAND,

INCLUDING THE MASSACRE OF AMERICAN PRISONERS,

DRAWN BY GLOVER BROUGHTON, 1815.

DARTMOOR PRISON, ENGLAND, embracing about 20 acres of land, is situated between the English and Bristol Chanels, fifteen miles from Plymouth. Prisoners landing at Plymouth, are huddled together like sheep and marched off to Dartmoor, under a Guard of Honor, resting occasionally till they arrive at the dreary, bleak and barren moor; not a tree or a shrub can be seen within three miles of its circumference. The Farmers term it the Devil's land, inhabited by Ghosts and sundry imaginary beings; they do not dare pass it by night. Rabbits cannot live there, and Birds fly from it.

The Prisoners passing through iron gates, enter the *dismal Stone Prisons* surrounded by two stone walls —Ditch and iron railing, the space between the railing and inner wall, is deadly green, seasoned with old bones, old shoes, cast of garments, &c., which create a sort of sensation. The yards are all roughly paved. A water course runs from the Reservoir without the wall, under ground through two channels—one to supply the Prisoners with water—the other passing under the outhouses connected with the ends of the prison next to the iron railing. There are seven Prisons built of rough stone and mortar, roofs all of slate, No. 1, 2, 3, 5, 6, 7, are separated from No. 4 by stone walls, within those Prisons, stancheons are fitted, similar to those in Stables for horses without partition. On these stancheons, hammocks are hung. Prisoners are divided into messes of six, each having a tin ticket numbered, to show when they call for their allowance of Bread and Beef, or salt herring instead of Beef, Barley soup and Vegetables. The floors are stone. always damp—windows, iron bars.

Those small houses attached to the Prisons were Cook houses, wherein dinner was provided for the Prisoners, no breakfast or supper, except eight ounces of bread. The Prisoners were turned out every pleasant morning by the Guard with muskets and fixed bayonets, for the purpose of having the Prisons swept and aired; if any were dilatory, the Guard would punch their bayonets against the hammocks, exclaiming—Turn Oot! Turn Oot! Many a poor mortal has turned out without sufficient clothing to protect him from the piercing wintry cold, health prostrated by the short allowance of food, and the dampness of the Prisons—chilled, would tremblingly move along, quiver and drop down dead. No. 4, was the special residence for colored Prisoners. The Snow in winter, has often covered the walls ten feet in height.— The Boxes painted blue in the yards and on the surrounding walls were for the Sentinels; at any moment those on the wall could pull a wire that would strike an Alarm Bell near the Barracks.

Prisoners, to drive dull care away, generally turned their attention to something, viz:—playing Ball, Dancing, Fencing, Boxing, keeping Schools, boiling Potatoes—Coffee—Teazan for a cold—Plaiting Straw for bonnets—Washing—Peddling. I, or Market Square, before the massacre, was used for the Prisoners accommodation, where those who had money, could go as far as the Iron Rail, and no further, to purchase Goods and Produce from the Jews and Country people, such as dry goods and produce, principally murphies. G, or Cashot, was for the special accommodation of all turbulent, ungovernable characters for heinous offences.

Five thousand Americans were imprisoned within those Walls. Five hundred were Marblehead men and lads—six hundred or thereabouts, were discharged from English Ships of War, impressed from the American merchant vessels, and compelled to serve on board those Bull Dogs, until the United States *demanded Free Trade* and *Sailors rights*, they then were paid off and confined among their countrymen, culled from Barbadoes, St. John, N. B., Halifax, St. John, N. F., Chatham and Plymouth, in that most detestable Dartmoor.

The massacre of the American Prisoners, by the Somersetshire Militia, Thomas George Shortland, commanding officer, was on the 6th day of April, A. D. 1815. The Prisoners were playing Ball opposite No. 7; unintentionally the Ball was knocked over the Wall into the Barrack Yard. The sentinel on the ramparts was requested repeatedly to throw it back, but refused. To gain the Ball a hole was broken through the wall—the alarm bell rang—then followed the Massacre, wherein seven were killed, sixty wounded.

In 1815, Great Britain acceded to the demands of the United States, a Treaty of Peace was signed, and the Prisoners returned to their Friends, to enjoy the blessings of a Second Independance.

The following extract from Roads' *History of Marblehead* illustrates how Marblehead was involved in the War of 1812.

During the spring of 1769, a brig belonging in Marblehead was boarded off Cape Ann by a lieutenant and a party of seamen from the British sloop-of-war Rose *and an attempt was made to impress some of the crew into the British service. A struggle ensued in which two of the Americans were severely wounded and the British lieutenant was killed by a blow from a harpoon thrown by one Michael Corbitt. At length, being overpowered by force of numbers, the brave men surrendered, and Corbitt was taken from Boston to be tried for murder.*

On Sunday afternoon, February 26, a British transport sailed into the harbor. Soon after a regiment of British soldiers, under the command of Colonel Leslie, landed on Homan's Beach. Suspecting the object of the expedition to be the seizure of several pieces of artillery secreted at Salem, the Marblehead regiment hastened to Salem to the North Bridge.

By the census of the year 1810, it appeared that the number of inhabitants of the town was 5842, of whom 63 were 'people of color'.

During the following year (1811) the town voted to 'purchase the tract of land at the entrance to the town, owned by Mr Aaron Waitt, at a price of not exceeding $3200; and to erect a suitable building for the permanent and convenient occupation of the poor of the town.'

On the 18th of June, 1812, war was formally declared against Great Britain by the Congress of the United States. The reasons publicly given for this step were substantially as follows: 'The impressment of American seamen by the commanders of the British ships of war; their doctrine and system of blockade; and the adoption and continuance of the Orders in Council, which operated extensively to the interruption and injury of American commerce.'

As soon as the news of the declaration of war was received in Marblehead, the town was the scene of the utmost activity. Four privateers, namely the Lion, *the* Thorn, *the* Snowbird, *and the* Industry *were immediately fitted out, and began a series of remarkably successful cruises against the ships of the British nation.*

This was not all. Forty private, armed schooners were soon fitted out in Salem, a large proportion of which were manned by Marblehead seamen. One schooner, the Growler, *was commanded by Capt. Nathaniel Lindsey, of Marblehead, and had an entire crew of Marblehead men. Of the crew of the ship* America, *one of the most conspicuous and successful cruisers during the entire war, thirty were from Marblehead.*

The fishermen of Marblehead were also largely represented on board the frigates of the United States Navy. Eighty men of the crew of the Constitution *were from Marblehead, and were on board her throughout the entire period of her brilliant career.*

Twenty-one citizens of Marblehead were impressed into the British naval service, namely: John Smith, William Hooper, John Holden, Thomas Curtis, Samuel Brimblecom, Philip Brimblecom, Richard Pearce, Paul Newhall, Israel Eaton, Benjamin Ashton, William Eaton, John Nicholson, William Homan, Thomas Mitchell, Jacob Wadden, Ambrose Dodd, William Mitchell, Lake Magan, Asa Prichard, William Pousland and Thomas Porter.

In the sea battle between the Guerriere *and the* Constitution *on August 19, 1812, the* Guerriere *lost one hundred one (101) in killed, wounding and missing. The loss on the* Constitution *was seven killed and seven wounded.*

On 29 December in 1812 a desperate engagement was fought off St Salvador between the United States frigate Constitution, *then commanded by Capt. Bainbridge, and the British frigate* Java, *of thirty-eight guns. The combat continued more than three hours, and when the* Java *struck, she was reduced to mere wreck. Of her crew one-hundred-and-sixty (160) were killed and wounded, while on board the* Constitution *there were only thirty-four. Among the killed on board the* Constitution *in this action were two brothers named Cheever, of Marblehead, the only sons of a poor widow.*

On 1 June, 1813, a battle was fought in the bay back of Marblehead Neck, in sight of a multitude of anxious spectators, by the United States frigate Chesapeake, *commanded by Capt. Lawrence, and the British frigate* Shannon, *commanded by Capt. Broke. The action terminated fatally for the* Chesapeake, *and the intrepid Lawrence was mortally wounded. Of the crew of the* Shannon, *twenty-four were killed and fifty-six wounded. Of the crew of the* Chesapeake, *forty-eight were killed and nearly one hundred (100) wounded. When carried below and asked if the colors should be struck, Capt. Lawrence replied, 'No, they shall wave while I live.' Delirious from excess of suffering, he continued to exclaim, 'Don't give up the ship!' an expression consecrated by the people of Marblehead as the last words also, of the heroic Mugford, thirty-seven years before.*

On Sunday 3 April, 1814, the citizens were alarmed by the sudden appearance of three ships of war, which appeared to be sailing directly for Marblehead Harbor. It proved to be the frigate Constitution *which for three days had been chased by the British frigates* Tenedos *and* Endymion. *The* Constitution *succeeded in escaping from her pursuers, and, as she majestically sailed into the harbor, cheer after cheer rent the air, and from many a heart a prayer of thanksgiving went forth for the preservation and safety of 'Old Ironsides'. When about three miles out, the commander of the* Constitution *inquired if any of the Marblehead seamen felt competent to pilot the ship into harbor, 'Aye, aye, Sir!' was the answer from a score of volunteers, and from the number Samuel Green was selected, by whom the good ship was successfully brought in.*

In February 1815, a treaty of peace was ratified by Great Britain and the United States. Though peace was declared, over seven hundred (700) citizens of Marblehead were confined in British prisons. Halifax, Chatham, Plymouth and the loathsome prison ships each had their own quota, while in Dartmoor Prison alone more than five hundred (500) were confined. The majority of these men were captured in privateers by British ships of many times their size and armament. Many, however, were taken from unarmed merchant vessels on their voyages to and from various foreign ports.

Over one thousand (1000) men from Marblehead were engaged in the war for 'free trade and sailors' rights'. Of these, seven hundred twenty-six (726) were on board privateers, one hundred twenty (120) were in the navy, fifty-seven were in the army, and one hundred (100) were members of the Marblehead Light Infantry.

At the close of the war there were only forty-eight vessels employed in the Bank fishery, eighteen of which were of less than fifty tons' burden. When the embargo of 1807 went into operation, there were one hundred sixteen (116) vessels engaged in the business, ninety-eight of which were of more than fifty tons' burden.

A member of the crew of the *Growler* by the name of Francis Selman also wrote a book called *Extracts from the Journal of a Marblehead Privateersman Confined On Board British Prison Ships 1813, 1814, 1815* on his return from captivity at Dartmoor. It was included in the *Marblehead Manual*, compiled by Samuel Roads Junior and published in 1883, and makes fascinating reading.

The following is part of Francis Selman's record. (Additions in brackets are by the author, taken from the general entry books of Dartmoor Prison, to help identification.)

1814. Friday, Sept. 9, The commander of this ship has found out that David Perry has swam away, and has kept us all down in the pound and threatened to fire amongst us, which we told him he was afraid.

Saturday, Sept. 10, At 5am the commander of this ship informed us we must get all our things on deck so as to go on board the Crown Prince, *which we did, and went alongside; but the commander of her would not let us come on board, and we had to return on board the* Bahama. *At ½ past 8 the men that were on board the* Crown Prince *came on board that ship. Amongst them was Mr Rust, who informed me that the exchange of prisoners had taken place, and that Capt. Lindsey had received a letter from home dated the 10th of June.*

Monday, Sept. 19, The commander of the ship informed us that two cartels were coming up the river to take the American prisoners to the United States.

Wednesday, Sept. 21, The clerk of this ship informed me that a cartel was expected here daily for the soldiers.

Saturday, September 24, The American soldiers signed the parole to return to the United States.

Sunday, Sept. 25, At 4am turned to be the sound of the drum. At noon went on board the Lyden 64, *bound to Plymouth.*

Monday, Sept. 26, All the prisoners on board all ready for sailing. At 3, got under weigh for Sheness. At 6, anchored at the Nose.

Tuesday, Sept. 27, At 2am, got under weigh. At 6pm, came to in the Downs.

Wednesday, Sept. 28, At 4pm, got under weigh with a fine breeze. Sixty allowed to go on deck at a time.

Thursday, Sept. 29, At 4, took a fine breeze from the east. At 4, hove to, blowing heavy, not safe to run.

Friday, Sept. 30, At 7, bore away. At 10am, came to in Plymouth Sound. Three Americans made their escape from this ship. Two got caught and one got clear.

Sunday, Oct. 2, Three Americans made their escape, Ferguson and Johnson and Eaton. Eaton was drowned; Johnson caught.

Friday, Oct. 7, At daylight ordered on deck. At 9am loaded and marched for Dartmoor Prison.

Francis Selman's details were recorded in the general entry book at Dartmoor Prison and read as follows:

Dartmoor Prison number	4436
By what ship or how taken	HMS Electra
Time when	*7 July 1813*
Place where	*at sea*
Name of prize	Growler
Man-o'-war, privateer, merchant vessel	*Privateer*
Prisoner's name	*Francis Selman*
Quality [rank]	*2nd Lieutenant*
Time when received in custody	*8 October 1814*
From what ship or how received	*Chatham Hulks*
Place of nativity	*Marblehead*
Age	*28*
Stature	*5ft 5ins*
Person	*Stout*
Visage and complexion	*Round, dark*
Hair	*Brown*
Eyes	*Blue*
Marks or wounds	*None*
Date of supply [goods, bedding]	*20 September 1814*
Exchanged, discharged, died, escaped	*Discharged*
Time when	*27 April 1815*
Whither and by what order if discharged	*Boards Order*
Date of order	*16 March 1815*

So hundreds of seamen and many ships came out of Marblehead and I have been lucky enough to befriend the descendants of three of these gallant men, firstly Mrs Marjorie Mace whose great-great grandfather was a seaman on the *Alfred.*

The *Alfred,* commanded by Captain Williams, was a brig of 16 guns and a crew of 130 men. She sailed from Salem on 16 August 1812 and one of her first prizes was the brig *Diamond* of 220 tons and 12 guns. She had a full cargo of cotton and log wood from Brazil and $2500 in gold. Another prize taken on the trip was the brig *George* of 270 tons which carried a cargo of sugar and cotton from Brazil. Together the *Diamond* and the *George* were valued at $120 000. The two brigs were sent into Salem.

The next brig taken was the *Terilla,* laden with fish from St John and bound for Bermuda. She was taken and burned at sea. The next to be taken was the brig *Curfew* with a cargo of fish and oil from Nova Scotia bound for St Lucia. It was sent into Marblehead. On 23 February 1813 the *Alfred* was three months out on her last cruise when she was spotted, chased and captured by the English sloop-of-war HMS *Epervie*r off Newfoundland. Her crew was taken to the war prison in Halifax and incarcerated there.

About half of the *Alfred*'s crew, 75 men, were shipped to Dartmoor at the time when American prisoners were being concentrated there. They were put aboard HMS *President* and arrived at Dartmoor on 30 September 1814. They were subsequently released on 4 June 1815 with the following exceptions:

3663 *Wm Blackler, released 10 April 1815*
3664 *Rich Goss, released 11 July 1815*
3757 *Benj Brown, aged fourteen, released 28 May 1815. This was about a week before the main crew were released, perhaps because of his age.*
3756 *John Kelley, died 29 March 1815 and was buried at Dartmoor. John Kelley was born in 1753 in Marblehead.*

William Stacey went home with the main body of the *Alfred*'s crew. He immediately resumed his career at sea, serving on several ships from 1815 until 1841 when he was put on the brig *General Ryan*. In 1849 he served aboard the *Marcia Cleaves,* followed by service on the *Sapphire*. This ship, of which he was captain, foundered in the West Indies on 8 March 1842 while on a voyage from Salem to Mobile. He continued to live a very eventful life. In 1850 he took passengers to San Francisco during the gold rush, in the hope of making some money for himself.

He was recommended for a position as an officer on the Nautical School Ship in Boston but was appointed inspector at Marblehead Custom House, staying in that post until he retired. The author has visited his house in Marblehead and stood before his grave with his great-great granddaughter to salute him with the Stars and Stripes flying. As previously recorded, Marjorie Mace and her daughter, Connie Blake, who is the great-great-great granddaughter of Stacey, visited for a tour of the prison at Dartmoor.

Captain William Stacey's grave in Marblehead (left), *and the author standing by the grave* (above).

The second friendship established was with Joan and Stan Von Sternberg. Joan Sternberg (née Dodd) had six ancestors in the War of 1812, three of whom were held at Dartmoor Prison. Two were seamen, both called Samuel Dodd. One served aboard the US vessel *Spitfire* before being taken to the Dartmoor Depot where he was given the prison No. 62, which means he was in the first group of Americans ever to be sent there, arriving on 2 April 1813. He was released two years later on 13 April 1815 and went home to Marblehead to continue his career as a seaman on vessels out of the port.

The crew of the Spitfire, recorded in the general entry books, were marched up to Dartmoor Prison on 2 April 1813 and were among the first Americans held at Dartmoor Prison, as can be seen by their prison numbers:

Prison No.	Name	Age	Rank	Place of Birth
53	Charles Lanson	23	2nd Mate	Beverly
54	Thomas Carton	26	Carp.	Pennbrook
55	William Bishop	17	Steward	Marblehead
56	Richard Wheller	23	Cook	Marblehead
57	Thomas Bartlett	21	Seaman	Marblehead
58	Francis Jones	38	Seaman	Marblehead
59	Fred Vic Jones	21	Seaman	Marblehead
60	John Jervis	21	Seaman	Marblehead
61	Thomas Wooldridge	19	Seaman	Marblehead
62	Samuel Dodd	17	Seaman	Marblehead
63	Fred Bridge	32	Seaman	Marblehead
64	Nicolas Witherham	27	Seaman	Marblehead
65	Benj. Jutt	22	Seaman	Marblehead
66	Jas. Dolliver	21	Seaman	Marblehead
67	Wm Lovet	21	Seaman	Marblehead
68	Jacob Wadden	39	Seaman	Marblehead
69	William B. Fletcher	45	Seaman	Marblehead

The crew of the *Spitfire* were all released from Dartmoor on 27 May 1815 after spending more than two years in captivity, with the following exceptions:

53	*Sent to the Chatham hulks on 27 May 1813*
55	*Sent to Mill Prison, Plymouth, on 10 July 1813*
61	*Released on 6 May 1814*
68	*Escaped on 10 Feb 1815*

Another of Joan Von Sternberg's ancestors was a seaman named Richard Winchester who was serving on the *Firefly* when captured and was sent to the Chatham hulks. He did not make it home, dying of fever on 9 March 1814. Details of Richard Winchester taken from the general entry books of the Chatham hulks:

Chatham hulk no.	2857
Name	Richard Winchester
Ship	Firefly *82 tons*
When captured	Captured at sea 19 Oct 1813 by HMS Revolutionaire
Place of birth	Salem
Age	22
Height	5ft 6ins
Stature	Strong
Visage	Oval – sallow
Hair	Brown
Eyes	Grey
Marks or wounds	Scar on right hand

Had Richard Winchester not died, he would have been transferred to Dartmoor along with all the American prisoners of war, in September 1814. The *Firefly*'s crew were sent first to the war prison at Halifax, then to the

Chatham hulks on 7 January 1814. I managed to trace some of the crew from my very incomplete records of the Chatham hulks:

2852	Wm Rowe	Seaman	Boston	27	
2852	Caleb Tar	Seaman	Mass.	26	
2853	Sam Pearson	Seaman	Mass.	24	
2854	David Allen	Seaman	Mass.	20	
2855	Josh Millett	Seaman	Mass.	39	
2856	Stephen Jones	Seaman	Mass.	18	
2857	Richard Winchester	Seaman	Salem	22	Died 9 Mar 1814
2858	Wm Williams	Boy	Mass.	14	
2859	John Day	Seaman	Mass.	30	
2860	Benj. Ellwell (2)	Mate	Boston	25	Died 18 Apr 1814
2861	Henry Shaw	Cook	Boston	23	
2862	Daniel Dempsey	Boy	Mass.	15	Died 12 Mar 1814

The clerks sometimes put the State as the place of birth instead of the town.

A fourth ancestor of Joan Von Sternberg's, to be held at Dartmoor was Cornelius Dodd who wrote the following letter home in 1814:

Kind Wife
I imbrace this opportunity to inform you that I am well and in good health. By the help and blessing of God and hopeing by the same blessing that these few lines will find you and all the Children in good health as you leave me at present.
I shall be glad to hear if you have heard any News from Corneis Dodd and if you can git his wages or any prospect of getting them for if you can get them I want to know to inform the Boatsman that [??] with them that voiage so I wish you to right to me as soon as posable and so doing you will obleage me. So no more at present. But remember me to all inquiring friends.
So I will close with saying I remain your faithful husband,
Cornelius Dodd.

There appears to be no information on Joan's other two ancestors, another Cornelius Dodd and Ambrose Dodd.

THE WILLIAM RICHARDSON STORY

I am grateful to the Marblehead Historical Society archives for the information on William Richardson.

Richardson and Thomas Tindley, both from the Marblehead area, served aboard privateers in the War of 1812, Richardson on the *America* and Tindley on the *Enterprise*. Both were first sent via Portsmouth to the Chatham hulks. Here follows part of the journal Richardson kept of his experiences, quoted verbatim from his written notes, though unfortunately they are incomplete:

Suffered severely, being reduced to a mere shadow by starvation, we arrived at Portsmouth the last day of December 1813. On the 1st January 1814 the 248 American prisoners, which were brought to England in the Diomede were transferred on board a tender brig and proceeded at once for the River Medway, nearly opposite Sheerness to Gillingham reach.
They chose this place because the prison ships were all located there, eight in number, viz the Glory [which] was a three-decker, she had principally been occupied by Danes, Swedes and American prisoners. She lay moored near a low bank which was used for a burial place, and formed a portion of Chatham harbor. She was afterwards hauled upon the bank. The second prison ship was the Bellauxcean, she was occupied by Swedes, and lay moored near the first, but had a turbulent commander. The third prison ship was the Sampson. She was occupied by about 900 French prisoners and lay moored near the entrance of Gillingham reach and those 248 American prisoners were thrust on board of her,

to mingle with French prisoners. They petitioned to the Transport Office Board making them known their situation, and if they were not relieved forthwith they indicated they would help themselves.
The fourth prison ship was the Crown Prince, *another turbulent…*[End of Richardson's notes Portsmouth to Chatham.]

When Richardson arrived at Chatham, he was given the hulk number 2990, his friend Thomas Tindley was given the number 2971, both numbers close together, indicating they were together when documented by English clerks.

On 8 October 1814 they were both sent on the *Leyden* ship to the Dartmoor Depot which at this time was used as a concentration prison for all American prisoners. Here follows more of Richardson's notes (all as written and spelt about his journey from the Chatham hulk *Bahama* to Dartmoor:

Taken from on board of the Bahama *by a brig tender and transferred to the* Leyden, *sails on the 3rd inst. for Plymouth, arrived there on the 5th and remained there two days, lost two men by drowning in trying to make their escape – one of them was named Josep Eaton of Beverly.*
Oct 8 the prisoners was tumbled on shore and placed under guard, and marched off to Dartmoor. The first notice we have of those 7 stone prisons we pass through 7 iron gates arrived at just before night and placed in No. 7 prison, the next day we were removed to No. 5 where we remained until the 15 of June 1815 when we were drafted to go home in a Dutch ship and sailed for Boston the next day. Why the English nation should have selected the most gloomy and unhealthy spot in their dominion to locate their prisoners, we know not what reply to give unless they are more crewil and barbarous than any other nation on earth, for meanness and niggardliness they are the most contemptible people, speaking symbolically of the race here is what one of their own race said about them…
Talk no more about your British bravery, no more of your genius boast since all your manly spirits are… [End of Richardson's journey to Dartmoor Prison from Chatham hulk.]

William Richardson was given the Dartmoor No. 4509 and Thomas Tindley 4493 when they arrived on 8 October 1814 – again the two numbers were close. Both were discharged on 15 June 1815. In 1835, twenty years after the massacre, the British Government renewed its proposal to grant pensions to all prisoners wounded in the massacre of 6 April 1815. As Richardson had seen Tindley being wounded by the militia, he was called upon by a justice of the peace as a witness. Being his messmate (i.e. shipmates) and knowing all the facts, he signed the affidavit and subsequently Tindley received $3000 back pay in 1835. This sum divided by 20 meant he received about $150 per year back pay, about three dollars per week for life. It is not known if the pension was ever raised.

In 1863 a book was published called *Historical Collections of the Essex Institute* which gave lists of ex-Dartmoor prisoners still living in the Salem, Lynn, South Danvers, Danversport, Beverly, and, of course Marblehead, at the end of 1853. The Marblehead list shows that Tindley was still alive and kicking and enjoying a British Government pension. There were 42 Marbleheaders still alive in that year, not all receiving pensions, of course.

Richardson's thoughts on the later events, in hand-written notes as before, are also still held with the Marblehead Historical Society (spelling as his notes):

The British Government having had time in their coold deliberation to reflect upon this sad event, examined into the whole affair, and as they found no motives for the prisoners to brake jail, they came to the wise conclusion to exonerate them from blame, and to show their sense of justice, they issued proposals to the American Government to grant pensions to all the prisoners who were wounded at Dartmoor.

The British Government in this transaction be it to their everlasting honor, acted more consistent and magnanimous than our own Government did towards priva-

teersmen, though they was benefited grately by their service. In conclusion I now refer back to the 9 page for the purpose to make a few casual remarks upon the characteristics of Joseph Furness, an impressed seaman from Marblehead into the British service in 1812… [End of notes.]

William Richardson's hand-written notes.

In 1860, Richardson, now sixty-five years old and described as a painter, started up a newspaper which he called the *Scorpion*. In the first edition, dated 11 October 1860, published in Marblehead Massachusetts, he described his newspaper as, 'a journal devoted to the interests of the privateersman'. In the *Scorpion* he placed his thoughts on the massacre, as a witness, on record. He must have seen John Washington killed by the militia, as he goes into detail as to how he was killed. He presumably also knew Washington quite well as he states that his parents were still living and that he had a sister. As we have already seen, Richardson was also a witness to Thomas Tindley being injured during the massacre.

MARBLEHEAD'S PRIDE

Over 1000 men from Marblehead were engaged in the War of 1812 for Free Trade and Sailors' rights', a proud record, indeed:

726 were on board privateers
120 were in the US Navy
57 were in the US Army
100 were members of the Marblehead Light Infantry

When some of the Marbleheaders were released and sent home on a cartel ship, it is stated that the captain was a man of timid nature, and would not order a full spread of sail, perhaps to preserve his masts and rigging. So the Marbleheaders went to him and politely explained that they would now crew the ship back home.

John Hubbard of Marblehead was selected to be the captain and ordered the full spread of sail, which hurried them home to freedom in the least possible time to meet their families waiting on the quayside.

The United States Navy was founded in Marblehead when five schooners called *Franklin, Handcock, Hannah, Lee* and *Warren* were commissioned by orders of General Washington in 1775, the first US Navy vessels to engage the enemy in warfare.

Some Marbleheaders were soldiers in what is now Canada, one being a man named Edward Latham who was thirty years old and serving with the American 14th Regiment when captured by British forces in Canada. He was sent to the Chatham hulks and given the number 3111; he, like Richard Winchester, succumbed to fever and was buried there.

Marblehead's role is also illustrated in these extracts from the *Western Flying Post*:

14 February 1814
Arrived at Plymouth the American schooner Hannah *from Marblehead bound for Nantz with salt fish. Captured by the frigate HMS* Andromache. *Also arrived on 4 February 1814 the American schooner* Joseph *from Marblehead. Captain Brown in command bound for France a prize to the brig* Royalist.

Plymouth 15 July 1814
On Saturday arrived the American privateer Rattlesnake *18 guns, nine days out from Rochelle by His Majesty's frigate* Hyperion. *Some Marblehead men amongst the American crew.*

Port News Plymouth *18 November 1814*
The cartel Saint Phillip *bound for America with American prisoners on board.*

So it is clear that Marblehead played a key part in many different ways throughout the war. My friends there have made visible to me the sorrow that would have prevailed during the years that so many men were kept prisoner. The absolute pride and loyalty surrounding these men lives on in the appreciation of their ancestors. I am sure that many small American towns feel the same loss and pride; my account for Marblehead stands for all towns involved in the war.

Plaque commemorating the founding of the US Navy in Marblehead.

Chapter Eight

THE UNITED STATES DAUGHTERS OF 1812

During the last 100 years an organisation called the United States Daughters of 1812 has, most patriotically, donated large sums of money to Princetown Church and Dartmoor Prison. In 1910 its members presented a magnificent stained-glass window to St Michael's Church, Princetown, and in 1928 the American Memorial Arch and plaque for the entrance to the American cemetery on prison land to commemorate the prisoners of war who died and are buried on Dartmoor. They have also donated money for maintenance to St Michael's. On 28 May 1928, Guy Burrage, Commanding Officer of US Naval Forces in European waters, came to Plymouth aboard the United States Scout Cruiser *Detroit* and attended the unveiling of the Memorial Arch.

In 1930 the US Daughters of 1812 presented the granite-mounted gravestone of Captain Allen of the *Argus*, later killed in action with HMS *Pelican* during the War of 1812, to the Prysten Chapel at the rear of St Andrew's Chapel in Plymouth. The Door of Unity was also presented here, the place that also commemorates midshipman Delphy, aged eighteen, killed in the same action. On the membership certificates of the Daughters is a picture of St Michael's Church, Princetown.

In the 1920s a prisoner at Dartmoor convict prison wrote a book called *Dartmoor from Within*. In it he tells of how he was once employed in the prison cemetery keeping it in good order and states that 'periodically a group of Americans visit the American cemetery to pay homage to the men who died so long ago'. He speaks of how he saw an old lady kneeling at the monument and later found a bunch of roses that she had left there.

During my fifteen years or so as prison historian I hosted several visits by the US Daughters of 1812 and on some occasions I managed to get the prison band to supply a bugler to blow the Last Post at the service held in the cemetery. In 1987 we had a major official visit at which I was presented with the emblem of the US Daughters of 1812, a star and anchor, which I had the pleasure of personally fitting to the American obelisk.

The last visit was made by Mrs Rynell Novak, chairman of St Michael's Preservation Committee in 1998. I hosted the visit and together we attended the church to see the sun shining through the magnificent stained-glass window, and to inspect all the items donated over the years for the interior. I applaud the Daughters for their patriotic actions and generosity and would advise anyone visiting Princetown to visit St Michael's Church to glory over the wonderful east window and see the artefacts presented over the years: the framed dedication of the 1910 east window; the parchment listing States which contributed to the window; a tablet presented in 1987 to commemorate a visit by the Daughters to the church and the American cemetery on prison land; and the flags of France, America and Great Britain.

The design of the east window is traditional and the caption to the photograph on the following page explains what each of the seven panels in the stained-glass window represents.

The window in St Michael's Church, Princetown, presented by the US Daughters of 1812 in 1910.

Panels 1 to 6, left to right, panel 7 at top:

1 *The Annunciation – Gabriel appearing to the Virgin.*
2 *The Madonna with infant child in arms.*
3 *Christ the Great Healer, healing a sick man.*
4 *Christ the Great Teacher, teaching small children.*
5 *The Crucifixion, Christ on the cross unattended.*
6 *The Resurrection.*
7 *The Ascension.*

ABOVE INFORMATION COURTESY OF
DEVON RECORD OFFICE, EXETER,
ACCESSION 5720A/PB1 TO PB16
PHOTOGRAPH BY AUTHOR

Above: *American, French and British flags in St Michael's Church, Princetown.*
Right: *An external view of St Michael's Church, taken in the 1940s. The building is no longer used for church services and is currently being renovated as part of a community project for Princetown.*

Left: *The American Memorial Arch presented by the US Daughters of 1812, May 1928.*
Above: *Detail of the plaque on the archway.*

Above: *The Presentation Ceremony, 30 May 1928. The picture shows Admiral Burrage and staff at the dedication service.*
Left: *A plaque presented by the US Daughters of 1812 and installed on the wall inside St Michael's Church to commemorate their official visit on 29 May 1987.*

Above: *A member of the author's staff, Bernard Sinclair, about to drill the obelisk prior to fitting in 1987 the Star-and-Anchor emblem of the US Daughters of 1812.*
Right: *The obelisk before drilling.*

Right: *The newly-attached emblem.*
Far right: *Picture about five years later to show the weathering of the bronze emblem.*

Chapter Nine

ENGLISH-BORN PRISONERS OF WAR

Several American prisoners wrote accounts of their time at Dartmoor Prison, Charles Andrews's account being the one to which I have most referred. It was certified by 62 men who were also prisoners. One of these men was Charles Bennett, an English-born American prisoner of war. Originally from near Manchester, his date of birth is given as 14 July 1785. He was thirty years old when he signed the certificate as Captain Charles Bennett, one of many Americans born in Great Britain who had emigrated to the United States during its years of infancy.

Sarah Bennett Reichart, a direct descendant of Charles Bennett, visited the prison with her husband, and her brother and his wife and gave the author this account of Bennett's life which she wrote in 1993:

Charles Bennett, mariner, was born on 14 July 1785 and was baptised on 28 September 1785 in the parish church of St Michael's in Ashton-under-Lyme which is about ten miles west of Manchester, England. His father was John Bennett who was a hatter by trade but was also skilled in cabinetry. In 1794 John Bennett decided to leave England and emigrate with his wife and children to America.

Family historical records state that he refused to pay a new tax on what he called 'God's light of day' which was the window tax imposed to raise money to fight the war against France. The Bennett family came to New Hudson, New York, a town founded barely ten years before. John Bennett found work making bricks from Claverack Creek and built a two-storey house there for the family. He also established a hatting business with easy access to beaver pelts from the Native Americans.

New Hudson was a seafaring town and ships were built here with a large trade overseas. Whalers, etc were in great demand. Charles Bennett went to sea in about 1800, aged fifteen. When the War of 1812 broke out he was serving on a merchant vessel called Marmion *which was captured by His Majesty's frigate* President *on 13 August 1813 off Nantes, France. He was sent to Dartmoor as a prisoner of war.*

On reception the following was noted. He gave his birthplace as New York city because if he had given his real birthplace in England he would have been hanged at the yardarm for treason. He was twenty-seven when captured and five feet, six-and-a-half inches tall. He was of sturdy build with an oval face, light complexion, brown hair and grey eyes. During the early part of the War of 1812 John Bennett had sent his sons away as he could not bear the thought of them fighting against Englishmen. He was loyal to America, however, and furnished funds to help the country.

Charles Bennett ran away on a vessel to fight against England. He was released on cessation of hostilities in 1815 and continued his life at sea. He spent the last twenty years of his life at Sailors Snug Harbour, Staten Island, New York. He died in 1861 and was buried in grave number 465 in the old cemetery at Sailors Snug Harbour which closed in the 1970s. All records were transferred elsewhere and many were lost. The records that were eventually found started at number 661, all preceding numbers being unfortunately lost, so the last resting place of this English-born American prisoner of war held at Dartmoor Prison during the War of 1812 cannot be traced.

Charles Bennett's details taken from Admiralty records (ADM 103/87):

Prison number	649
By what ship or how taken	HMS President
Place where	Marmion
Man-o'-war, privateer merchant vessel	Merchant vessel
Name	Charles Bennett
Quality [rank]	2nd mate
Time in custody [Plymouth hulks]	31 August 1813
Received at Dartmoor	8 September 1813
Whence received	Plymouth
Place of nativity [birthplace]	New York
Age	27
Stature	5ft 4ins
Person	Stout
Visage, complexion	Oval, fair
Hair	Brown
Eyes	Grey
Marks or wounds	None
Exchanged, discharged died or escaped	Discharged
Time when	Wed 26 April 1815
By what order	Boards Order 16 March 1815

Above: *Sarah Bennett Reichart and her husband, with her brother and his wife in the American cemetery.*

Above right: *Sarah Bennett Reichart and her brother, direct descendants of an American prisoner of war, Charles Bennett, who was one of the signatories of Charles Andrews's journal, stating it was a correct account, and the only journal kept. Charles Bennett was English, born and bred near Manchester.*

Chapter Ten
LIFE AFTER THE WAR

The story did not end for those prisoners who made it back home after their gruelling experiences. It is interesting to know what happened to them when life returned to normal; take, for example, one Francis Dolphin of Baltimore, his story told courtesy of his great-great-great grandson Richard Elmer Johnson.

The general entry books of Dartmoor Prison (ADM 103/91) contain these details:

Prison Number	*6063*
By what ship or how taken	*HMS* Recruit
Time when	*6 April 1814*
Place where	*Lat 29 Long 76 (Charlestone Light)*
Name of Prize	Chasseur
Man-o'-war, privateer, merchant vessel	*Privateer*
Quality [rank]	*Seaman*
Time received in custody	[at Dartmoor] *28 Dec 1814*
From what ship	*HMS* Penelope
Place of nativity [birthplace]	*Bordeaux*
Age	*20*
Stature	*5ft 3ins*
Person	*Stout*
Visage/complexion	*Oval/ dark*
Hair	*Brown*
Eyes	*Grey*
Marks or wounds	*Some smallpox scarring, and scar left leg*
Date of supply, 1 hammock, 1 bed, 1 blanket	*28 Dec 1814*
Exchanged, discharged, died, escaped	*Discharged*
Time when	*3 July 1815*
Whither, and by what order if discharged	*Boards Order 16 March 1815*

Additional information was supplied by Richard Elmer Johnson. Dolphin was aboard the British schooner *Lark*, which had been captured by the privateer *Chasseur* a few days before. He was part of an eight-man prize crew from the *Chasseur*, out of the port of Baltimore, Maryland, and nicknamed the *Pride of Baltimore*. After the *Chasseur* had taken the *Lark* as a prize of war, the ships were headed for an American port when the *Lark* was recaptured by the English man-of-war HMS *Recruit*. The seven men with Francis Dolphin were: Hugh McDongall, Kemp Southcombe, Barnet Duffel, Alex Dove, John Nichols, John Marion and George Moore. They were all brought to the Dartmoor Depot on 28 December 1814 and finally released on 3 July 1815.

On his release from Dartmoor, Dolphin went back to Baltimore, where, on 1 January 1824, he married Henrietta A. Baldwin, born 23 May 1803 in

Alexander, Virginia. They had four children: Eliza Jane, born 1826, Francis Wheeler, born 1831, Francis Emma, born 1840, and Virginia, born after 1840.

In 1853 he applied for the post of inspector of beef and pork, and his application gives some details of his employment beforehand:

To the authorities Baltimore 30 Jan 1853, the Mayor and other officers.

This is to certify that Francis Dolphin of this city of Baltimore is well known to us, who is an applicant for a licence as Inspector of beef and pork under the Ordinance of the Mayor and city councils, and that he is capable of the said situation, having been for many years a labourer and deputy inspector of provisions.

John D. Early

Nine further signatories signed to say they fully concurred with the above.

When Francis died on 15 October 1863, a report appeared in the *American and Commercial Advertiser*:

Death of a Dartmoor Prisoner, Mr Francis Dolphin died at his residence in Mulberry Street, near Pine, on Thursday in the 71st year of his life. The deceased was one of the oldest meat-packers in this city, where he resided for the last fifty-seven years. His life was an eventful and honorable one; a native of Bordeaux, France, he emigrated in early life with his family to St Domingo, where he miraculously escaped being a victim to the terrible massacre there.

He subsequently came to Baltimore and served in the War of 1812, during that war he was one of those captured on board the armed brig Chasseur *(fitted out in the port of Baltimore), conveyed as prisoner to England and incarcerated in Dartmoor Prison, until liberated by the treaty peace of 1815. Only two others of those confined at the time with Mr Dolphin, are now residents of this city. The recital of his experiences whilst a prisoner in the notorious Bastile was deeply interesting, and calculated to arouse the indignation of every patriotic heart.*

On 28 May 1889 his widow Henrietta applied for a service pension as follows:

Claimant alleges her husband served three years in the naval service, enlisted at Baltimore on the US brig Chasseur, *was captured by the enemy, and was incarcerated in Dartmoor Prison in England, liberated on the termination of the war.*

The answer was:

Third edition reports that there are no rolls of the Chasseur *on file, so rejected on the ground of no such service be alleged.*

Henrietta's application was rejected because the *Chasseur* was not a US Navy vessel but a privateer, and privateers were not eligible for pensions from the US Government. Henrietta died on 25 February 1892, also in Baltimore.

Opposite: Returned prisoner of war, Francis Dolphin, acted as a witness to an application, and his signature is at the bottom of the document.

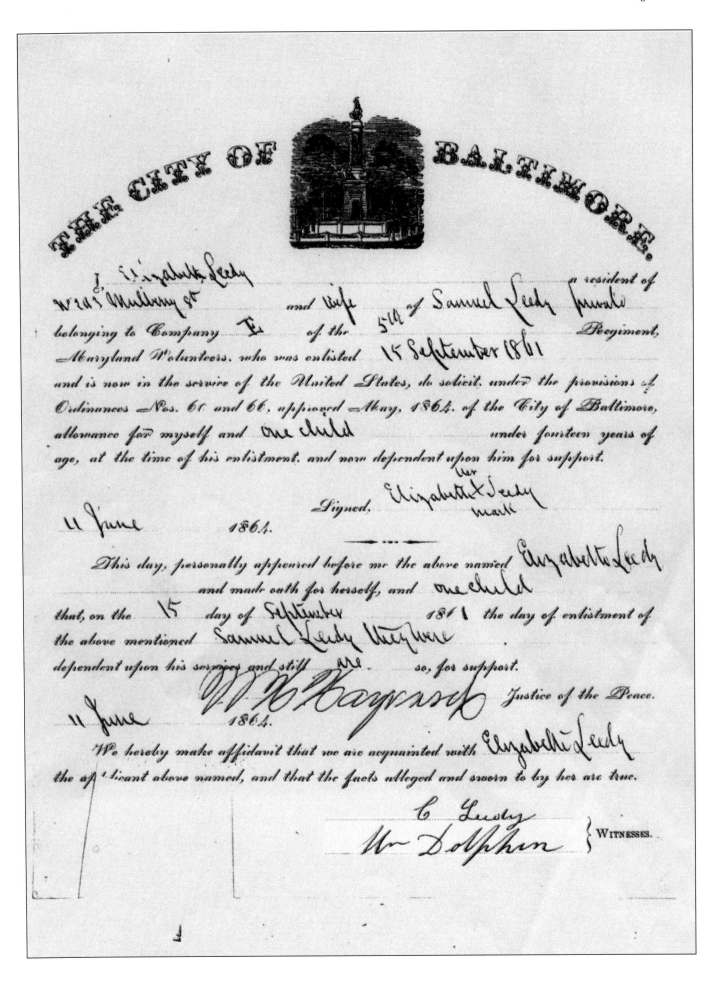

Returned prisoner Francis Dolphin's successful application for the post of meat inspector at Baltimore, dated 30 January 1853 (see page 104).

Chapter Eleven
THE BOY WHO LIES BURIED

John Seapatch was twelve years old when he was taken prisoner in the War of 1812, marched to Dartmoor and died there less than two months later:

Dartmoor Depot number	5889
By what ship or how taken	Bulwark
Time when	*23 Nov 1814*
Place where	*off Halifax*
Name of prize	Harlequin
Man-o'-war, privateer,	
merchant vessel	*Privateer*
Prisoner's name	*John Seapatch*
Quality [rank]	*Boy*
Time when received into custody	*27 Dec 1814*
From what ship or how received	HMS Penelope
Place of nativity [birth place]	*Massachusetts*
Age	*12*
Stature	*4ft 9ins*
Person	*Middle size*
Visage/complexion	*Oval/fair*
Hair	*Light*
Eyes	*Grey*
Marks or wounds	*None*
Date of supply [bedding etc]	*27 Dec 1814*
Exchanged, discharged, died,	
escaped	*Died*
Time when	*7 Feb 1815*

Why was this very young boy not put ashore on the eastern seaboard of the United States and told to make his way home to a no-doubt worried mother?

Over about fifteen years or so as the prison historian, whenever passing by, the author would always pick a wild flower, put it on the obelisk in the American cemetery and say, 'Sleep well John Seapatch, America is proud of you.'

At the end of April 1815, 263 ragged Americans left Dartmoor Prison and marched to Plymouth, and from there to freedom. They left behind over 5000 fellow prisoners who would, over time, themselves complete the long march to the cartel ships in Plymouth docks. The men who marched away carried a large flag on which there was a representation of the Goddess of Liberty sorrowing over the tomb of the Americans who died. It bore the inscription 'Colombia weeps and will remember'.

Before the men left the prison they thanked Dr McGrath for his kindness by giving an address. They spoke highly of the tall, thin, one-eyed McGrath but called his assistant, McFarlane, a monster. By July 1815 most of the Americans, except those in hospital, had left and the very last prisoners of war, 4000 Frenchmen taken at Ligny came into Dartmoor. They were considered much easier to handle than the Americans. After a short period, the war with France had again ended and by February 1816 the majority of the prisoners had left Dartmoor. By early summer all the sick men in the hospital were fit enough to be sent home.

The forbidding fortress that had witnessed more than 9000 French and American prisoners pass through its bleak granite walls – or die within them never to see their native land again – fell eerily silent. Dartmoor's wilderness once more reclaimed its own as Tyrwhitt's grim edifice stood empty until the time, some thirty-four years later, when it would open its doors again, to become one of the world's most infamous convict prisons.

Appendix One

THE FIRST PRISONERS

The first 250 Americans who were marched up to Dartmoor on 2 April 1813.

Prison No.	Name	Unit/Ship	Date first captured	Place of birth	Age
I	Michael Towers	Impressed	8 Jan 1813	Hingham	27
2	Richard Smith	*Cashier*	3 Feb 1813	New York	23
3	Saml Spear	ditto	ditto	Boston	26
4	John Mullan	ditto	ditto	New York	23
5	Wm Deal	ditto	ditto	Bell Haven	17
6	Rob Hallpenny	ditto	ditto	Baltimore	19
7	Fred Sharman	ditto	ditto	ditto	19
8	Thom. Wood	ditto	ditto	Prince George's County	21
9	Jos Gallaway	ditto	ditto	Talbot County	21
10	And. Birch	ditto	ditto	Baltimore	19
11	Josh Jentle	ditto	ditto	New Ob [?]	28
12	Joachim Riceo	ditto	ditto	Lima	28
13	Edward Blackman	ditto	ditto	New Tharse	23
14	Thom. Gilbert	ditto	ditto	Philadelphia	52
15	Henry Drake	ditto	ditto	New York	23
16	Rufus Hodge	ditto	ditto	Massachusetts	22
17	Henry Evans	ditto	ditto	Philadelphia	29
18	Th. March	ditto	ditto	NewYork	32
19	John Kimmins	ditto	ditto	ditto	25
20	Fred Madden	ditto	ditto	Alexandria	19
21	Rueben West	*Tyger*	8 Aug 1812	Falmouth	21
22	John Newell	ditto	ditto	Africa	32
23	Uriah Atkins	ditto	ditto	Burtown	26
24	John Hubbard	ditto	ditto	Philadelphia	29
25	Len Leeds	ditto	ditto	Boston	18
26	Lar Blanchard	ditto	ditto	Milford	21
27	Eben. Hough	*Alligonney*	ditto	[?] Dale	22
28	John Odeen	ditto	ditto	Alexandria	21
29	Harry Warner	ditto	ditto	New Haven	28
30	Brook Berry	ditto	ditto	Prince George County	20
31	Wm Conway	ditto	ditto	Marblehead	22
32	Geo Higgins	ditto	ditto	Boston	24
33	John Mires	ditto	ditto	Stalsound	24

34	John Glover	*Phoenix*	8 Aug 1812	Massachusetts	35
35	Josh Hovey	ditto	ditto	ditto	32
36	Josh Foster	ditto	ditto	Beverly	23
37	Josh Vankeak	ditto	ditto	Wheeland	23
38	Hoanse Paterson	ditto	ditto	Salem	17
39	Wm Barnes	Howard	8 July 1812	Pheboth	26
40	Rob Burnes	ditto	ditto	ditto	23
41	John Lovet	*Terrible*	8 Feb 1813	New Jersey	40
42	In Smith	ditto	ditto	Graton	23
43	Peter Martin	ditto	ditto	Arlington	24
44	Barney Kronhaut	*Terrible*	ditto	Baltimore	23
45	Eliakam Root	ditto	ditto	H [?]	20
46	Eldridge Smith	ditto	ditto	Poundstown	28
47	Zacearn Tufts	ditto	ditto	Hamilton Hampton	28
48	Will Leach	ditto	ditto	Derby	20
49	Wm Smith	ditto	ditto	New York	18
50	Jas. Cook	ditto	ditto	ditto	25
51	Wm Williamson	ditto	ditto	Bridport	15
52	Prince Freeman	HMS *Boyne*	14 Feb 1813	Bus [?]	34
53	Ch. Lanson	*Spitfire*	ditto	Beverly	23
54	Thomas Carton	ditto	ditto	Penbrook [?]	26
55	Wm Bishop	ditto	ditto	Danvers	17
56	Rich Wheller	ditto	ditto	Marblehead	23
57	Tho. Bartlett	ditto	ditto	ditto	21
58	Fran Jones	ditto	ditto	ditto	38
59	Fran Vic Jones	ditto	ditto	ditto	21
60	John Jervis	ditto	ditto	ditto	21
61	Thom. Wooldridge	ditto	ditto	ditto	19
62	Sam Dodd	ditto	ditto	ditto	17
63	Fr. Bridge	ditto	ditto	ditto	32
64	Nicolas Witherham	ditto	ditto	ditto	21
65	Ben Jutt	ditto	ditto	ditto	22
66	Ja. Doliver	ditto	ditto	ditto	21
67	Wm Lovet	ditto	ditto	ditto	21
68	Jacob Wadden	ditto	ditto	ditto	39
69	Wm B. Fletcher	ditto	ditto	ditto	45
70	Henry Mills	*Rolla*	11 Feb 1813	Georgetown	29
71	J. Williams	ditto	ditto	Salem	19
72	I. Johnson	ditto	ditto	New York	23
73	Jn Morris	ditto	ditto	ditto	28
74	Wm Ryan	ditto	ditto	Philadelphia	19
75	Jas. Ireland	ditto	ditto	Egg Harbour [?]	28
76	Wm Armstrong alias John Casey	ditto	ditto	New York	27
77	Sam Bright	ditto	ditto	Pecsham [?]	26
78	Jn Rotner	ditto	ditto	Philadelphia	25
79	Ja. Reeves	ditto	ditto	Salem	25

80	A. Augustin	*Rolla*	11 Feb 1813	New Orleans	47
81	Ed Johnstone	ditto	ditto	Darlington, England	68
82	Fra. Lessall	ditto	ditto	Sebastion	22
83	Ant Colcocha	ditto	ditto	New Orleans	26
84	Gm Caulle	ditto	ditto	Philadelphia	14
85	Josh Bloom	*Cashier*	3 Feb 1813	Pennsylvania	25
86	John Longworthy	ditto	ditto	New Burn	41
87	In. Harris	ditto	ditto	Newland	25
88	K. Inbritson	ditto	ditto	ditto	22
89	Geo. Bannister	ditto	ditto	New England	23
90	Dan Cooper	ditto	ditto	Baltimore	30
91	Abr. Pack	ditto	ditto	Harford	26
92	Sam Shamson	ditto	ditto	Baltimore	35
93	Wm P. Jones	*Paul Jones*	9 Feb 1813	H [?] Hill [?]	35
94	Jas Grey	ditto	9 Feb 1813	Richmond	20
95	Ant. Woodward	Paul Jones	ditto	Philadelphia	17
96	Wm Elles	ditto	ditto	Chads Island	17
97	Isaac Covell	ditto	ditto	Ellington	29
98	Ant L. Allen	ditto	ditto	Gloucester	21
99	Darius Mains	ditto	ditto	Georgetown	24
100	Isaac Russel	ditto	ditto	New Jersey	24
101	Michel Hulet	ditto	ditto	Shrewsbury [?]	21
102	Whitny Thompson	ditto	ditto	Hartford	23
103	Alex Merrit	ditto	ditto	Blandford	21
104	Geo. Taylor	ditto	ditto	New Jersey	27
105	John Gilbert	ditto	ditto	New York	20
106	David Morrison	ditto	ditto	Philadelphia	30
107	Peter Wills	ditto	ditto	Norwich	29
108	Sam Athroun	*Rolla*	11 Feb 1813	Philadelphia	30
109	In. Fosten	HMS *Tophound*	2 Apr 1813	Boston	23
110	Rob. Anderson	ditto	ditto	Rhode Isles	26
111	Jas Evans	ditto	ditto	Charlestown	30
112	Ignasious Parsons	ditto	ditto	Gloucester	24
113	Thomas Grey	*Rolla*	11 Feb 1813	Baltimore	28
114	Jas Boffs alias Boggs	*Gov McKean*	ditto	Londonderry Island	62
115	In. Baptist	ditto	ditto	New Orleans	21
116	Andrew Lehens	ditto	ditto	Murport [?]	25
117	Barth Capewell	ditto	ditto	New Orleans	25
118	Jon. Regens	ditto	ditto	Salem	25
119	Jon. Hook	ditto	ditto	Pennsylvania	24
120	Fran Farrott	ditto	ditto	Philadelphia	23
121	S. Harps	ditto	ditto	Virginia	19
122	Php White	ditto	26 Jan 1813	Pennsylvania	17
123	Peter Winter	ditto	ditto	Newcastle	25
124	Jac Humphries	ditto	ditto	Philadelphia	28
125	Amos Augustus	ditto	ditto	Wilmington	17

126	Ben S. Davis	*Good Intent*	26 Jan 1813	Gloucester	26
127	Sam. Al. Sargant	ditto	ditto	Cape Ann	20
128	Jas. Mellett	ditto	ditto	ditto	21
129	Thom. Andrews	ditto	ditto	Marblehead	21
130	In. Dobins	*Williams Transport*	ditto	Hartford	27
131	Job Brewster	*Mars*	26 Feb 1813	Duakbury [?]	22
132	In. Johnson	*Criterion*	14 Feb 1813	Rhode Island	23
133	Arch Thomas	ditto	ditto	New York	25
134	John Miller	ditto	ditto	Queen Ann's County	25
135	Martin Thompson	ditto	ditto	Deusport [?]	36
136	In. Royal	ditto	ditto	Peters Forrugh	28
137	Jabez Marble	ditto	ditto	Massachusetts	23
138	Thom. Griffiths	ditto	ditto	New York	31
139	Ch. Dickson	ditto	ditto	ditto	24
140	Henry Cramber	ditto	ditto	Oldenburg	24
141	David Neel	ditto	ditto	Philadelphia	27
142	In. Schulz	ditto	ditto	Stralshound [?]	20
143	Rich Manett	ditto	ditto	New York	26
144	Wm Barron	ditto	ditto	ditto	25
145	Thom. Bidson	ditto	ditto	ditto	22
146	Moses Sage	ditto	ditto	Middletown	29
147	In. Dewett	ditto	ditto	New York	18
148	Wm Reeves	ditto	ditto	Westchester	16
149	Henry Brown	ditto	ditto	New York	17
150	Ch. Ludlow	ditto	ditto	New Jersey	17
151	In. Harry	HMS *Abercrombie*	[?]	New Orleans	45
152	Wm Fawcett	HMS *Lavinia*	2 Apr 1813	Peterborough	29
153	Wm Fossendor	ditto	ditto	Husbury [?]	24
154	Wm McLelland	ditto	ditto	Schenacty [?]	30
155	Jas. Staitmaud	ditto	ditto	Salisbury	25
156	Jos. Matthews	ditto	ditto	Rhode Island	30
157	Cato Foster	ditto	ditto	Marblehead	33
158	Amos Pierce	ditto	ditto	Newhamptonshire [?]	29
159	Wm. Johnson	Prisoner of war	[?]	New York	26
160	Thad. B. Starbuck	Impressed	7 Jan 1813	Nantucket	24
161	Asay Whitehouse	ditto	ditto	Brickfield	23
162	Geo. Brown	*Full Blooded Yankee*	9 Mar 1813	Millfleet	37
163	Washington Fox	ditto	ditto	Alexander	38
164	Oliver Rock	ditto	9 Mar 1813	Morlaix	34
165	In. Allen	Impressed	10 Jan 1813	Richmond	23
166	Steph. Check	ditto	ditto	County of Kent Del.	31
167	Geo. Dingall	Flag of truce/Pennsylvania	10 Jan 1813	Maryland	28
168	In. Eddy	ditto	10 Jan 1813	Hampton	18
169	Thom. Gilbert	Impressed	15 Jan 1813	Norfolk	50
170	David Flood	ditto	10 Feb 1813	Portland	25
171	Wm Allen	*Brazilian*	18 Dec 1812	Boston	35
172	Sam. Rosett	Impressed	23 Feb 1813	New York	31

173	Alex Petterson	Impressed	23 Feb 1813	ditto	29
174	Josh Rhoderick	*Hope*	15 July 1813	St Mary's	39
175	Wm Thomas	ditto	15 July 1813	New Orleans	35
176	In. Crete	ditto	15 July 1813	ditto	24
177	Ch. Smith	HMS *Mackerel*	[?]	Albany	26
178	Dan Holts	*Star*	9 Feb 1813	New London	24
	alias Hops				
179	Wm Mallery	ditto	ditto	New Orleans	32
180	In. Hughes	ditto	ditto	Philadelphia	26
181	Joshua Right	ditto	ditto	Saysbrook [?]	24
182	Wm Erwin	ditto	ditto	Cumberland	33
183	Judeth Dennison	ditto	ditto	Saysbrook [?]	25
184	Peter Duston	ditto	ditto	New York	19
185	Sam. Romain	ditto	ditto	ditto	30
186	Gersham Jonstone	ditto	ditto	ditto	26
187	Wm Thompson	ditto	ditto	Copenhagen	23
188	Tho. Gordon	ditto	ditto	New Orleans	22
189	Josh Richman	ditto	ditto	Maryland	21
190	Moses Isaac	ditto	ditto	New York	21
191	Wm Clerk	ditto	ditto	Newport	19
192	Gab. Borgin	ditto	ditto	Somerset County	17
193	Tho. Vaughan	ditto	ditto	New York	21
194	Hampton Sullivan	ditto	ditto	Wilmington	19
195	Jas. Trash	ditto	ditto	New York	24
196	In. C. Clements	ditto	ditto	New Jersey	23
197	F. Joseph	ditto	ditto	New Orleans	20
198	Edw. Washburn	ditto	ditto	New York	20
199	H. Lowring	ditto	ditto	Norfolk	35
200	In. Valentine	ditto	ditto	New York	17
201	Wm A. Mix	ditto	ditto	New Haven	18
202	Horace Bisley	ditto	ditto	Rockhill	18
203	In. Cox	ditto	ditto	Chester	20
204	H. Williams	ditto	ditto	New Orleans	35
205	In. Lewes	ditto	ditto	Staten Island	18
206	Ch. Wheeler	*Criterion*	14 Feb 1813	Smithstown [?]	36
207	In. Monks	ditto	ditto	Massachusetts	39
208	Wm Porter	ditto	ditto	Rhode Island	25
209	H. White	ditto	ditto	Maryland	21
210	Jas. Lawson	*Mars*	26 Feb 1813	Africa	27
211	Benj. Jones	ditto	ditto	Washington	25
212	Geo. Parker	ditto	ditto	New York	25
213	Ant. Barret	ditto	ditto	New Orleans	58
214	In. Baker	ditto	ditto	Baltimore	25
215	Jas. Caldwall	ditto	ditto	West Nottingham [?]	28
216	Ch. Whitewood	ditto	ditto	New York	28
217	Henry Allen	ditto	ditto	Vermont	21
218	Wm Saunders	ditto	ditto	Massachusetts	19

219	Wm Smith	*Pert*	1 Mar 1813	New York	26
220	Wm Ware	ditto	ditto	Philadelphia	38
221	In. Treddle	ditto	ditto	Long Island	28
222	Tho. Lawson	ditto	ditto	Stanford	36
223	Wm Gellens	ditto	ditto	Philadelphia	20
224	Robt Court	ditto	ditto	ditto	19
225	Wm Hull	ditto	ditto	New York	31
226	Reub. Stoddart	*Charlotte*	ditto	Massachusetts	17
227	Peter Norman	ditto	ditto	Talunsville [?]	36
228	Wm Brown	ditto	ditto	New York	30
229	And. Holmes	ditto	ditto	ditto	21
230	H. Sammers	ditto	ditto	ditto	23
231	Wm Forbes	ditto	ditto	Boston	20
232	Alex Christy	ditto	ditto	Charlestown	25
233	Ch. Davis	ditto	ditto	Norfolk	27
234	Jas. Goff	ditto	ditto	New York	22
235	John Pike	ditto	ditto	Washington	18
236	Jas. Taylor	ditto	ditto	Philadelphia	24
237	Zek. Mitchell	ditto	ditto	Massachusetts	23
238	Wm Akens	ditto	ditto	New London	23
239	Geo. Williams	ditto	ditto	Maryland	24
240	Miles Cox	*Orbit*	29 Jan 1813	Philadelphia	29
241	Geo. Blanchard	*Wm Bayard*	3 Mar 1813	Elizabeth Town	21
242	In. Roe	ditto	ditto	New Orleans	27
243	Loring Averill	ditto	ditto	Con [?]	19
244	In. Mather	ditto	ditto	Philadelphia	27
245	Rob Barlow	ditto	ditto	Pennsylvania	33
246	In. Lewes	ditto	ditto	New York	20
247	An. Sinnott	ditto	ditto	Philadelphia	34
248	Ben Jones	ditto	ditto	Milford	27
249	William Finch	*Unicorn*	17 Jan 1813	Orange County	25
250	Geo. C. Gorling	*Wm Bayard*	3 Mar 1813	[?]	18

Appendix Two

MEN FROM MARBLEHEAD HELD AT DARTMOOR

Prison No.	Name	Unit/Ship DD = Died E = Escaped	Date captured	D = Discharged	Date	Age
31	Wm Conway	*Alliganny*	8 Aug 1812	D	30 July 1813	22
56	Rich Weller	*Spitfire*	14 Feb 1813	D	20 Apr 1815	23
57	Thom. Bartlett	ditto	ditto	D	ditto	21
58	Fran. Jones	ditto	ditto	D	ditto	38
59	Fran. Vic Jones	ditto	ditto	D	ditto	21
60	John Jervis	ditto	ditto	D	ditto	21
61	Thom. Wooldridge	ditto	ditto	D	ditto	19
62	Samuel Dodd	ditto	ditto	D	ditto	17
63	Fra. Bridge	ditto	ditto	D	ditto	32
64	Nic Witheram	ditto	ditto	D	ditto	27
65	Ben Jutt	ditto	ditto	D	ditto	22
66	Jas. Dolliver	ditto	ditto	D	ditto	28
67	Wm Lovet	ditto	ditto	E	10 Feb 1815	21
68	Jacob Wadden	ditto	ditto	D	20 Apr 1815	39
69	Wm B. Fletcher	ditto	ditto	D	16 July 1813	45
129	Thom. Andrews	*Good Intent*	20 Jan 1813	D	30 July 1813	21
373	Wm Griffin	*Independence*	16 Mar 1813	D	20 Apr 1815	20
469	Jas. Eastland	*Essex*	2 Apr 1813	D	ditto	35
470	Sam Bencroft	ditto	ditto	D	ditto	29
525	Edw. Giles	*Friends*	15 July 1813	D	26 Apr 1815	26
764	Glover Broughton	*Pallas*	3 Nov 1813	D	ditto	17
768	J. Bude Mason	ditto	ditto	D	ditto	22
890	R. Dolliver	*General Kempt*	18 Dec 1813	D	27 Apr 1815	19
986	Jn Ramsden	*Hannah*	15 Jan 1814	D	ditto	14
1023	Wm Hammond	*Joseph*	18 Jan 1814	D	ditto	22
1025	Wm Stacey	ditto	ditto	D	ditto	21
1026	Phillipe Besson	ditto	ditto	D	ditto	18
1027	Elias Chambers	ditto	ditto	D	1 May 1815	13
1106	W.B. Orne	*Bunker Hill*	4 Mar 1814	D	27Apr 1815	29
1111	Ebenezer Graves	ditto	ditto	D	ditto	24
1244	Wm Hooper	HMS *Elizabeth*	7 Aug 1812	D	26 Apr 1815	33
1282	Phillip White	*Indian Lass*	29 Apr 1814	D	28 Apr 1815	30
1476	Wm Maine	*Essex*	20 Apr 1813	D	1 May 1815	20

1528	Henry White	*Essex*	20 Apr 1813	D	ditto	24
1529	Tho. Moss	ditto	ditto	D	ditto	44
1574	Tho. Clothey	ditto	ditto	D	ditto	20
1593	J. Hammond	*Eliza*	27 Mar 1813	D	ditto	22
1616	Fran Jeffrey or Trefry	*Essex*	2 Apr 1813	D	ditto	17
1635	Peter Trefry	ditto	ditto	D	ditto	26
1667	Mark Murrell	*Shadow*	6 Apr 1813	D	ditto	29
1711	Andrew Peal	HMS *Urgent*	8 July 1814	D	ditto	22
1767	James Farrell	*Cygnet*	8 Mar 1814	D	ditto	20
1770	George Knight	*Print*	21 Jan 1813	D	ditto	25
1771	John Dolabar	ditto	ditto	D	ditto	33
1772	Wm Knight	ditto	ditto	D	ditto	19
1773	Fran Sweet	ditto	ditto	D	ditto	24
1774	Robt B. Ireson	ditto	ditto	D	ditto	15
1798	Nath. Rogers	*Polly*	23 Mar 1813	D	ditto	23
1833	William Harris	*Lightening*	2 Apr 1813	D	ditto	43
1846	Josh Egoss	*Polly*	23 Mar 1813	D	ditto	14
1858	Cha. Williams	*Volante*	25 Mar 1813	D	2 May 1815	21
1893	John Domeree or Tillinan	*General Kempt*	18 Dec 1813	D	ditto	21
1909	Thomas Courtis	HMS *Mars*	28 Oct 1812	D	26 Apr 1815	37
1935	Thomas Mitchels	HMS *Royal William*	3 Feb 1813	D	2 Apr 1815	35
2108	Wm Hammond	*Thetis*	11 June 1814	D	2 May 1815	26
2266	Wm Griffin	*Siouyo* [?]	27 May 1814	D	3 May 1815	49
2400	George Pedrick	*Frolic*	20 Apr 1814	D	19 Oct 1814	24
2401	Bent Hammond	ditto	ditto	D	ditto	23
2402	G.A. Horton	ditto	ditto	D	ditto	35
2404	Stacey Curtis	ditto	ditto	D	ditto	23
2408	Josh Benson or Beazon	*Frolic*	ditto	D	ditto	23
2410	Mich Carroll	ditto	ditto	D	ditto	23
2436	Wm Chambers	ditto	30 Aug 1814	D	2 May 1815	22
2580	Sam Chine	*Print*	21 Jan 1813	D	26 Apr 1815	25
2595	Josh Delabar	*Rachael*	2 Dec 1812	D	26 Apr 1815	44
2596	John Howman	ditto	ditto	D	ditto	27
2618	Jonas Howman	ditto	9 Feb 1813	D	3 May 1815	27
2657	Nath Lee	*Growler*	7 July 1813	D	19 May 1815	12
2659	Josh Grush	ditto	ditto	D	ditto	21
2674	Jn Bartlett	*Joseph*	2 June 1813	D	ditto	24
2690	Jacob Johnson	*Porcupine*	3 June 1813	D	ditto	22
2694	Tho. Brush	*Industry*	3 Nov 1813	D	ditto	54
2723	M.C. Lemon	*John of Salem*	6 Feb 1813	E	23 Oct 1813	33
2801	Tho. Dennis	*Registator*	10 June 1813	D	19 May 1815	23
2827	Sam Blumbloem	HMS *Monmouth*	15 July 1813	D	ditto	40
2979	Wm Woolridge	*Frolic*	25 Jan 1813	D	ditto	16
2932	John Greaves	HMS *Berwick*	24 Aug 1814	D	ditto	34
2984	Geo. Jackson	*Frolic*	25 Jan 1815	D	ditto	25

3255	Burrel Whitham	*Growler*	7 July 1813	D	28 May 1815	23
3273	W.W. George	*Rachael*	9 Feb 1813	D	ditto	20
3280	Wm Clark	*Montgomery*	5 May 1813	D	ditto	25
3281	Wm Wanton	ditto	ditto	D	ditto	32
3289	John Widger	*Enterprize*	21 May 1813	D	ditto	27
3290	Peter Melzard	ditto	ditto	D	ditto	20
3292	John Clothy	ditto	ditto	D	ditto	41
3293	Rob Russell	ditto	ditto	D	ditto	38
3294	Fred Williams	ditto	ditto	D	ditto	21
3295	Jesse Goss	ditto	ditto	D	ditto	18
3296	Wm Clothy	ditto	ditto	D	ditto	34
3303	Abm Francis	*Porcupine*	3 June 1813	D	ditto	34
3375	Wm Bowden	*Growler*	7 July 1813	D	ditto	17
3376	Josh Windyer	ditto	ditto	D	ditto	21
3377	Will Russell	ditto	ditto	D	ditto	19
3381	Ben Brown	ditto	ditto	D	ditto	21
3383	Sam Threshow	ditto	ditto	D	ditto	26
3384	Tho. Roundy	ditto	ditto	D	ditto	26
3421	Israel Ekton	*Industry*	3 Nov 1813	D	ditto	37
3422	Sam Tucker	ditto	ditto	D	ditto	21
3423	Rob Burridge	ditto	ditto	D	ditto	46
3424	John Inglas	ditto	ditto	D	ditto	25
3425	John Gowaller	ditto	ditto	D	ditto	32
3426	Wm Bartell	ditto	ditto	D	ditto	38
3427	Louis Russell	ditto	ditto	D	ditto	21
3430	John Stacey	ditto	ditto	D	ditto	37
3433	Josh Sloper	*Growler*	7 July 1813	D	ditto	23
3436	Paul Newel	HMS *Astrea*	18 Nov 1813	D	ditto	22
3448	Ben Laskey	*Industry*	3 Nov 1813	D	ditto	18
3451	Chas Florance	*Growler*	7 July 1813	D	ditto	56
3594	Thomas Stevens	*Frolic*	25 June 1814	D	4 June 1815	28
3609	John Hooper	*Martha*	6 Feb 1814	D	ditto	22
3654	John Grush	*Growler*	7 July 1813	D	ditto	30
3659	Josh Northey	*Industry*	Sept 1813	D	ditto	19
3663	Wm Blackler	*Alfred*	23 Feb 1813	D	10 Apr 1815	28
3664	Rich Goss alias Josh Martin	ditto	ditto	D	4 June 1815	31
3665	Ben Graham	ditto	ditto	D	ditto	28
3666	Josh W. Green	ditto	ditto	D	ditto	20
3668	John Broughton	ditto	ditto	D	ditto	22
3669	Wm Thomson	ditto	ditto	D	ditto	28
3670	Samuel Roff	ditto	ditto	D	ditto	53
3671	Fred Bowden	ditto	ditto	D	ditto	30
3672	Josiah Thomas	ditto	ditto	D	ditto	24
3673	Wm Ryan	ditto	ditto	D	ditto	22
3674	John Patten	ditto	ditto	D	ditto	21
3676	Ben B. Gale	ditto	ditto	D	ditto	23

3677	Fra. Roundy	*Alfred*	23 Feb 1813	D	ditto	21
3678	Job Hunt	ditto	ditto	D	ditto	25
3679	Merrit Brumblowcum	ditto	ditto	D	ditto	48
3680	Stephen C. Rounder	ditto	ditto	D	ditto	19
3682	John Techant	ditto	ditto	D	ditto	63
3683	John Pierce	ditto	ditto	D	ditto	16
3684	Josh Barker	ditto	ditto	D	ditto	21
3685	Peter Savary	ditto	ditto	D	ditto	20
3686	John Carrivell	ditto	ditto	D	ditto	25
3687	Osmon C. Stacey	ditto	ditto	D	ditto	19
3688	John Bessop	ditto	ditto	D	ditto	16
3690	Edw. Hammond	ditto	ditto	D	ditto	18
3691	Tho. Vickery	ditto	ditto	D	ditto	18
3692	Wm Brown	ditto	ditto	D	ditto	21
3693	Sewel [?] Brimblecomb	ditto	ditto	D	ditto	22
3696	Rob Woolridge	ditto	ditto	D	ditto	19
3697	Sam L. Roundy	ditto	ditto	D	ditto	18
3698	Mich Corbett	ditto	ditto	D	ditto	20
3699	John Proctor	ditto	ditto	D	ditto	23
3700	Rob. Prichard	ditto	ditto	D	ditto	21
3701	Henry Lane	ditto	ditto	D	ditto	47
3704	Andrew Nowland	ditto	ditto	D	ditto	17
3705	Jacob Waite	ditto	ditto	D	ditto	63
3706	Prince Prince	ditto	ditto	D	ditto	24
3707	Oliver Francis	ditto	ditto	D	ditto	17
3708	Ez. Leech	ditto	ditto	D	ditto	18
3709	David Gilbert	ditto	ditto	D	ditto	18
3711	Ben Hawks	ditto	ditto	D	ditto	19
3713	Nat. Fuller	ditto	ditto	D	ditto	24
3715	Ambrose Rogers	ditto	ditto	D	ditto	20
3716	Isaac Warden	ditto	ditto	D	ditto	20
3717	Dan Chapman	ditto	ditto	D	ditto	54
3718	John Bunyan	ditto	ditto	D	ditto	23
3719	John Davis	ditto	ditto	D	ditto	40
3724	Sam Carroll	ditto	ditto	D	ditto	15
3725	Wm Stacey	ditto	ditto	D	ditto	17
3754	Ben Pittman	ditto	ditto	D	ditto	49
3755	Ben Pritchard	ditto	ditto	D	ditto	18
3756	John Kelly	ditto	ditto	DD	29 Mar 1815	62
3757	Ben Bowden	ditto	ditto	D	28 May 1815	14
3758	Rich Lee	ditto	ditto	D	4 June 1815	52
3759	John Cole	ditto	ditto	D	ditto	19
3760	Edw. Hammond	ditto	ditto	D	ditto	19
3858	James Thompson	*Prometheus*	June 1814	D	9 June 1815	19
3884	Walter Bastard	*Rattlesnake*	11 July 1814	D	ditto	20
3972	Charles Veal	ditto	ditto	D	ditto	55
3980	John Garney	ditto	ditto	D	ditto	26

4009	Abr Allen	*Rattlesnake*	13 July 1814	D	ditto	54
4010	Wm Dennis	ditto	ditto	D	ditto	40
4036	John Read	ditto	ditto	D	ditto	22
4039	John Bruce	ditto	ditto	D	ditto	47
4042	John Florence	ditto	ditto	D	13 June 1815	48
4046	Tho. Bowden	ditto	6 Oct 1814	D	ditto	29
4047	Wm Williams	ditto	13 July 1814	D	ditto	20
4048	Nath. Goldsmith	ditto	ditto	D	ditto	24
4052	Sam Chapple	ditto	ditto	D	ditto	20
4083	Edw. Selman	*New Zealand*	21 Apr 1814	D	ditto	28
4200	Israel Pritchard	*Hannah*	15 Jan 1814	D	ditto	22
4201	John Selman	ditto	ditto	D	ditto	19
4218	Edw. Derby	*Liberty*	30 Dec 1813	D	ditto	26
4353	Edw. Homan	*Plutus*	1 Apr 1814	D	14 June 1815	29
4370	John Smith	*Growler*	7 July 1813	D	ditto	25
4436	Fran Selman	ditto	ditto	D	27 Apr 1815	28
4437	Josh Brown	ditto	ditto	D	14 June 1815	29
4541	Andrew Tucker	ditto	ditto	D	15 June 1815	36
4542	Ben Pitman	ditto	ditto	D	ditto	21
4543	Mich Coombe	ditto	ditto	D	ditto	21
4544	George Foster	ditto	ditto	D	ditto	42
4545	Nath. Tucker	ditto	ditto	D	ditto	22
4546	Nath. Grush	ditto	ditto	D	ditto	17
4656	Jn Nicholson	ditto	ditto	D	ditto	23
4657	Wm F. Denny	ditto	ditto	D	ditto	22
4658	Jer. Smith	ditto	ditto	D	ditto	35
4667	Rob Blair	*Industry*	3 Nov 1815	D	ditto	22
4670	George Melzard	ditto	ditto	D	ditto	42
4671	David Ross	ditto	ditto	D	ditto	27
4672	Edw. Robes	ditto	ditto	D	ditto	15
4673	John Glover	ditto	ditto	D	ditto	18
4786	J.G. Hubbard	*Fame*	2 Sept 1813	D	21 June 1815	25
4790	Wm Dennis	*Frolic*	24 Jan 1814	D	11 July 1815	28
4901	Ben Russell	*Alfred*	23 Feb	D	21 June 1815	18
4902	James Kelley	ditto	ditto	D	ditto	23
5102	Tho. Colley	*David Porter*	12 Sep 1814	D	29 June 1815	26
5146	Fra. Burgess	*Thorn*	7 May 1813	D	ditto	19
5148	John Hammond	ditto	ditto	D	2 May 1815	19
5149	James Gros	ditto	7 Nov 1813	D	29 June 1813	36
5150	John Holden	ditto	ditto	D	ditto	15
5156	Rich Alston alias Nicholas Ashton	*Volante*	25 Nov 1813	D	ditto	21
5157	Corn Dotts	ditto	ditto	D	ditto	21
5158	Fra. Werrell alias Morrell	ditto	ditto	D	ditto	22
5185	John Henley	*Montgomery*	1 May 1813	D	ditto	53
5274	Wm Strong	*Swordfish*	28 Dec 1813	D	ditto	22

5278	Mich Joseph	*Growler*	7 July 1813	D	ditto	14
5302	John Fletcher	ditto	20 July 1813	D	ditto	22
5219	James Fulton	*Industry*	17 July 1813	D	ditto	15
5320	Js. Dullivan	ditto	ditto	D	ditto	16
5321	Tho. Jarvis	ditto	ditto	DD	25 Jan 1815	18
5324	David Blair	*Julia Smith*	10 May 1813	D	29 June 1815	22
5325	Ben Blair	*Enterprize*	21 May 1813	D	ditto	28
5326	John Peach	ditto	ditto	D	ditto	17
5384	Tho. Groves	*Rattlesnake*	17 Mar 1814	D	1 July 1815	21
5389	Jonah Bates	*Lister*	3 July 1814	D	ditto	22
5461	Tho. Cloutman	*General Putnam*	8 Nov 1814	D	ditto	39
5462	John Willison	ditto	ditto	D	10 Apr 1815	34
5485	Wm Killett	ditto	8 Dec 1814	D	1 July 1815	17
5490	Tho. Golliver	ditto	ditto	D	ditto	57
5494	Tho. Grant	*General Putnam*	8 Nov 1814	D	ditto	22
5495	Wm Burgen	ditto	ditto	D	ditto	46
5503	Lewis Orcroft	*Scorpion*	22 Aug 1814	D	ditto	34
5525	Wm Scobe	*Sally*	3 Aug 1814	D	ditto	16
5801	Joel Truffey	Gig	26 Aug	D	16 June 1815	26
5966	Edw. Homan	*Amazon*	22 Sep 1814	D	3 July 1815	57
5978	Sam Stacey	*Cossack*	1 Nov 1814	D	ditto	18
6115	Wm Dixey alias Tho. Collins	*Garland*	22 Nov 1814	D	11 July 1815	21
6208	Tho. Nowland	*Prince de Neufchatel*	28 Dec 1814	D	5 July 1815	22
5750	Stephen Stacey	*Ohio*		DD	12 Apr 1815	35
5537	Rich Rob Lee	*Ann*		DD	20 Jan 1815	23
4486	Josh Lackey	*Enterprize*		DD	4 Feb 1815	30

There were of course many more Marbleheaders. Glover Broughton of Marblehead, who would have known all the prisoners from the town, states that Dartmoor held 500 of its men at the same time. At least six of their number died at the prison and are buried there; there could be more as it appears that many men gave their birthplace as simply Massachusetts.

Appendix Three

CREW OF THE *ALFRED*

Crew members held at Dartmoor from William Stacey's ship, the *Alfred* (approximately half of the ship's total crew):

Prison No.	Name	Age	Rank	Place of birth
3661	Patrick Ryan	41	Master's Mate	Lucyford
3662	Wm Philp	28	Prize Master	Salem
3663	Wm Blackler	28	ditto	Marblehead
3664	Rich Goss	31	ditto	ditto
3665	Ben Graham	28	ditto	ditto
3666	Josh W. Green	20	Clerk	ditto
3667	Wm Richardson	20	Steward	Salem
3668	John Broughton	22	Prize Master	Marblehead
3669	Wm Thomson	28	Boatswain	ditto
3670	Samuel Roff	53	Gunner	ditto
3671	Fred Bowden	30	Gunner's Mate	ditto
3672	Josiah Thomas	24	ditto	ditto
3673	Wm Ryan	22	Sailing Mr	ditto
3674	John Patten	21	Seaman	ditto
3675	Mathew Wright	26	Quarter Mr	Ipswich
3676	Ben B. Gale	23	ditto	Marblehead
3677	Fra. Roundy	21	Seaman	ditto
3678	Job Hunt	25	ditto	ditto
3679	Merrit Brumblowcum	48	ditto	ditto
3680	Stephen C. Rounder	19	ditto	ditto
3681	Sam Conway	31	ditto	Salem
3682	John Techant	63	ditto	Marblehead
3683	John Pierce	16	ditto	ditto
3684	Josh Barker	21	ditto	ditto
3685	Peter Savary	20	ditto	ditto
3686	John Carrivell	25	ditto	ditto
3687	Osmon C. Stacey	19	ditto	ditto
3688	John Bessop	16	Boy	ditto
3689	John Smith	24	Seaman	Newberry
3690	Edw. Hammond	18	ditto	Marblehead
3691	Thomas Vickery	18	ditto	ditto
3692	Wm Brown	21	ditto	ditto
3693	Sewel [?] Brimbelcomb	22	ditto	ditto

3694	Sam Preston	20	Seaman	Salem
3695	Dan Cox	40	ditto	Delaware
3696	Rob Woolridge	19	ditto	Marblehead
3697	Sam Roundy	18	ditto	ditto
3698	Michael Corbett	20	ditto	ditto
3699	John Proctor	33	ditto	ditto
3700	John Prichard	21	ditto	ditto
3701	Henry Lane	47	ditto	ditto
3702	Kitt White	63	ditto	ditto
3703	Edward Tucker	19	ditto	Salem
3704	Andrew Nowland	17	ditto	Marblehead
3705	Jacob Waite	63	ditto	ditto
3706	Prince Prince	24	ditto	ditto
3707	Oliver Francis	17	ditto	ditto
3708	Ez. Leech	18	ditto	ditto
3709	David Gilbert	18	ditto	ditto
3710	John [?]	18	ditto	Cape Ann
3711	Ben Hawks	19	ditto	Marblehead
3712	Nat. Fuller	54	ditto	Ipswich
3713	John Pritchard	24	ditto	Marblehead
3714	Peter I. Cox	16	ditto	New York
3715	Ambrose Rogers	20	ditto	Marblehead
3716	Isaac Wadden	20	ditto	ditto
3717	Dan Chapman	54	ditto	ditto
3718	John Bunyan	23	ditto	ditto
3719	John Davies	40	ditto	ditto
3720	John Wakefield	54	ditto	Salem
3721	Titus Lane	30	ditto	ditto
3722	Ceazar Wilcox	42	ditto	Tumaho [?]
3723	George Storey	21	ditto	Marblehead
3724	Sam Carroll	15	Boy	ditto
3725	William Stacey	17	Seaman	ditto
3726	John Wilson	31	ditto	Salem
3727	Richard Ross	18	ditto	Savannah Creole
372X	Jonas Dennis	[?]	[?]	[?]
3754	Ben Pittman	49	Seaman	Marblehead
3755	Ben Pritchard	18	ditto	ditto
3756	John Kelly	62	ditto	ditto
3757	Ben Bowden	14	Boy	ditto
3758	Richard Lee	52	Seaman	ditto
3759	John Cole	19	ditto	ditto
3760	Edward Hammond	19	ditto	ditto

Appendix Four

AMERICAN DEATHS

The plaque on the American Memorial Arch at Dartmoor states that 218 American prisoners of war are buried there. However, there has never been a definitive list of prisoner deaths so I applied to the American group responsible for military cemeteries in England whose list also showed 218 names. Having found names to vary from list to list as I researched them, I was not satisfied with this. Then in 1992 and 1995 I visited the town of Marblehead, Massachusetts, to research their records of deaths from this period.

I checked Vol 4 *Vital Records* to 1850 and *Town Records* Vol 5, 10 March 1810 to June 1837. In record number 872 I discovered the name of William B. Fletcher who was born in Marblehead. He served aboard the US vessel *Spitfire* and died on 16 July 1813, and was recorded as buried at a prison in England. Yet he did not appear on the official list supplied by the American Military cemeteries authority. I wondered why there was no definitive list and which of the various records were correct. Without an accurate list, how can justice be done to the supreme sacrifices made by the men who died here? What can be worse than a man dying for his country unacknowledged?

It seems abhorrent that there are American prisoners of war buried at Dartmoor who have been completely forgotten. In 1995 I purchased some microfilm of the American general entry books at Dartmoor Prison and the first death I came across was that of the aforementioned William B. Fletcher. I have found many other names of men buried at Dartmoor yet omitted from the official list. While I cannot state my list to be definitive (not being certain that all possible records are to hand), there should certainly be more than 218 names on the plaque. Just twenty-four hours of study of the microfilms turned up 267 names. Later an American historian, Ira Dye, added four more, making a total of 271 Americans buried on Dartmoor Prison lands.

There are undoubtedly problems in compiling a final, complete list of the American, or French, prisoners who died at Dartmoor during the Napoleonic Wars and the War of 1812, and in naming with certainty the ships they served on. This is often because of the convoluted way in which they arrived at Dartmoor and what happened to them afterwards.

Take, for instance, the aforementioned Francis Dolphin who was on board an English schooner *Lark* which the American privateer called *Chasseur*, but nick-named the *Pride of Baltimore,* had captured a few days before. He was part of an eight-man prize crew from the *Chasseur*, taking the *Lark* to an American port when the *Lark* was recaptured by HMS *Recruit,* an 18-gun brig of war. All the American prisoners were taken to Plymouth, England by HMS *Penelope* and received at Dartmoor on 28 December 1814. The only thing that is certain is that he belonged to the crew of the *Chasseur* when taken so that is how I arrived at his ship, which may or may not be the ship he left America on.

The spelling of some prisoners' names varies and again it is possible to illustrate why. On entry of each prisoner, the clerks at the depot had to make some 30 separate entries for each individual. Even a small scar somewhere on the body would be recorded as an identifying mark. All this meant extreme pressure on the clerks when a large draft of French or American prisoners arrived, sometimes 2000 at a time!

At a later date one of those prisoners, take for example a man who might be called Jacob Moral, is taken ill and admitted to the hospital where the infirmary clerks, often prisoners helping out, record him as Jacob Morrell. He then dies in the infirmary, leaving behind uncertainty as to his correct name. Similarly a prisoner recorded as James Knabb, number 4871, was sent to the infirmary where he died and was recorded as William Knabbs. A third prisoner was entered as Thomas Jack on arrival at the depot and given the number 6520. He was shot during the massacre of 6 April 1815 and taken to the infirmary where he died the next day. He is recorded on 7 April 1815 as Thomas Jackson. My personal preference in cases such as these is to take the infirmary clerks' version, as they dealt with one prisoner at a time rather than the depot clerks who dealt with thousands. Admiralty records ADM 103/640 deal with these infirmary records.

I hope that the list I compiled helps in some way in the remembrance of the courageous men who died at Dartmoor. They each made a huge sacrifice in giving their life for their country during the War of 1812 and to record their name is the smallest but most important tribute.

AMERICAN DEATHS AT THE DARTMOOR DEPOT DURING THE WAR OF 1812
(Taken from ADM/103/87)

Dartmoor Depot General Entry Books – 1813 to 1815

Prison No.	Name	Unit/Ship	Date of death	Hometown	Age	Rank
69	Wm B. Fletcher	*Spitfire*	16 July 1813	Marblehead	45	Seaman
94	John Grey	*Paul Jones*	26 Apr 1815	Richmond	20	ditto
132	John Johnson	*Criterion*	1 Feb 1815	Rhode Island	23	Boatswain
182	William Erwin	*Star*	16 Mar 1815	Cumberland	33	Seaman
191	William Clerk	ditto	21 Oct 1813	Newport	19	ditto
202	Horace Bisley	ditto	11 Apr 1813	Rockhill	18	ditto
210	Jas Lawson	*Mars*	5 Jan 1814	Africa	27	Steward
218	William Saunders	ditto	16 Jan 1814	Mass.	19	Seaman
237	Ezekiel Mitchell	*Charlotte*	12 Jan 1815	Mass.	23	ditto
263	John Steel	*William Bayard*	15 Dec 1814	Maryland	26	ditto
298	Sam Robinson	*Ducornau*	15 Feb 1815	Boston	33	ditto
306	Nath Vaughan	ditto	31 Aug 1814	Newport	27	ditto
412	William Tyren	*Viper*	25 Feb 1814	Windall	21	ditto
414	Thomas Williams	ditto	20 Mar 1814	Conn.	23	ditto
430	George Jones	ditto	30 Apr 1814	New Orleans	24	ditto
443	Lamen Harris	*Magdalen*	5 Mar 1814	Mass.	20	ditto
482	Benj Rennaben	*Fox*	16 Nov 1813	New Orleans	28	ditto
486	John Roberts	Gave himself up	12 May 1815	Baltimore	28	ditto
488	Thomas D. Lippart	*Paul Jones*	9 Mar 1815	Penn.	49	Prize Master
491	Dumpy Kitre	ditto	23 Dec 1814	North Carolina	25	Seaman
555	Henry Freely	*Pompee*	20 Jan 1814	Penn.	29	ditto
572	James Henry	*Argus*	3 July 1814	New York	18	ditto
587	Thomas Baron	ditto	8 Nov 1813	Norfolk Va.	21	Servant
599	William Dillain	ditto	10 May 1814	New Guernsey	48	Marine
635	James Coombes	ditto	20 Mar 1814	Wicasset	22	Seaman
654	Henry More	*Marmion*	4 Jan 1814	New York	30	ditto
661	Aaron Peter	*Joel Barlow*	14 Jan 1815	Rhode Island	21	ditto
676	James Murray	*Messenger*	17 Oct 1813	Kent County	24	ditto
700	Josh Ranson	*Ned*	1 Mar 1815	Philadelphia	23	ditto
739	Henry Addigo	*Argus*	23 Dec 1813	New York	41	Soldier
743	Matthew Timerman	*Tom Thumb*	26 Sep 1814	New York	30	Seaman
754	John Montgomery	Impressed	24 Feb 1814	New York	21	ditto
788	Johnathan Dyer	*True Blooded Yankee*	11 Mar 1815	Cape Cod	40	
794	Elisha Toby	ditto	9 Mar 1814	Mass.	24	ditto
816	William Edgar	*Hepsa*	28 Jan 1814	New Jersey	36	ditto
829	Fran Romel	*Chesapeake*	7 Feb 1815	St Sebastian	26	ditto
838	Charles Cornish	ditto	10 Jan 1814	Maryland	40	ditto
840	Benjamin Cook	ditto	6 Apr 1814	Baltimore	26	ditto
851	Rich Schew	*Amiable*	8 Feb 1814	New York	32	ditto
892	Samuel Pass	*Dart*	12 Mar 1814	Not given	?	ditto
946	John Perkins	*Siro*	3 Nov 1814	Newhampton	25	Carps Mate

951	John Strout	*Siro*	20 Jan 1815	Portland	16	Seaman
953	William Thomson	ditto	18 Apr 1815	Port Prince	25	Cook
970	Jabez Mann	ditto	6 Apr 1815	Boston	30	Seaman
1038	William Shaw	*Argus*	17 Oct 1814	Philadelphia	23	ditto
1054	Ed Williams	Out of a Russian ship	21 Mar 1815	Virginia	22	ditto
1060	Joseph Butts	*Fair America*	2 Dec l814	New York	22	ditto

ADM 103/88

1113	James Gatwood	*Bunker Hill*	17 Feb 1815	Portsmouth	33	ditto
1131	James Badson	*Young Dixon*	22 Mar 1815	Boston	31	ditto
1140	William Diamond	*Mary Blockhead*	23 Jan 1815	Rhode Island	19	ditto
1162	Thomas Jackson	*Hebrus*	6 Jun 1814	New York	24	Cook
1253	John Cole	*Adeline*	26 Nov 1814	Baltimore	38	Seaman
1332	Thomas Peck	*Paul Jones*	15 Mar 1815	New London	39	ditto
1346	Manuel Martin	ditto	22 Sep 1814	New Orleans	17	ditto
1347	Joseph Took Johnson	ditto	6 Apr 1815	Conn.	19	ditto
1350	Charles Brown	ditto	17 Feb 1815	Virginia	23	ditto
1395	Daniel Carter	*Zebra*	6 Oct 1814	Virginia	26	ditto
1489	French Tutle	*Leo*	24 Nov 1814	Falmouth	26	ditto
1504	Abm. Thomas	*Paul Jones*	23 July 1814	Newhaven	32	ditto
1507	Sam Parish	*Grand Napoleon*	1 Apr 1815	Norfolk	31	ditto
1508	James Hart	*Courier*	8 July 1814	New London	28	ditto
1522	Benjamin Dilno	*Essex*	30 Mar 1815	Mass.	19	ditto
1523	Simon Chandler	ditto	25 Oct 1814	Mass.	19	ditto
1538	William Mills	*Zebra*	24 Mar 1815	New Jersey	21	ditto
1559	John Williams	*Caroline*	14 Jan 1815	Conn.	25	ditto
1578	James Roberson	*Price*	1 Apr 1815	Mass.	21	ditto
1608	James Baldwin	*Fox*	5 Dec 1814	Boston	24	ditto
1624	Andrew Smith	*Tom*	5 Mar 1815	Maryland	24	ditto
1636	Nathaniel Jenkins	ditto	21 Feb 1815	Baltimore	20	ditto
1649	Thomas Ricks	Taken in Bristol	22 Jan 1815	New York	26	ditto
1708	Thomas Hall	*Surprize*	18 Apr 1815	Maryland	36	ditto
1739	John Louis	*Hugh Jones*	5 Aug 1814	New Orleans	24	ditto
1752	John Marshall	*Alchinene*	8 Apr 1815	New Bedford	41	ditto
1768	Amos Larkin	*Reynard*	29 Jan 1815	Beverly	30	ditto
1780	Alex Henderson	*Criterion*	27 Dec 1814	Conn.	26	ditto
1920	William Johnson	*Antelope*	9 Mar 1815	Philadelphia	29	ditto
1922	Benjamin Babb	*Victory*	29 Jan 1815	Barrington	34	ditto
1934	William Beck	*Royal William*	18 Jan 1815	Portsmouth	50	ditto
1998	Johnathan Paul	Impressed	9 Mar 1815	Charlestown	30	ditto
2018	John Francis	*Royal William*	15 Apr 1815	Portsmouth	38	ditto
2027	Arch Fogerty	*Horatio*	18 Mar 1815	Fanstown	38	ditto
2094	George West	*Malta*	27 Jan 1815	Baltimore	24	ditto
2096	William Bean	ditto	28 Nov 1814	Virginia	34	ditto
2135	Francis Saul	*Mercurious*	20 Oct 1814	cannot decipher	32	ditto
2145	Tim Stanwood	*Aboukir*	20 Mar 1815	Newburyport	23	ditto

2225	Jacob Anderson	*Hussar*	26 Jan 1815	Portland	24	ditto
2240	Lewis Larkin	*Young Wasp*	30 Sep 1814	Conn.	24	ditto
2337	John Hopson	*Snapdragon*	14 Mar 1815	North Carolina	23	ditto
2351	Richard Miller	ditto	20 Nov 1814	Pennsylvania	26	ditto
2354	Josh Fulford	ditto	27 Jan 1815	North Carolina	22	ditto
2367	Simon Clark	ditto	24 Jan 1815	North Carolina	16	ditto

ADM 103/89

2418	Darius Belloa	*Frolic*	25 Jan 1815	Providence	29	ditto
2425	Dan Appleton	ditto	4 Jan 1815	Ipswich	28	ditto
2495	Edw. Norton	ditto	29 Sep 1814	Mass.	21	ditto
2541	James Gayler	*America*	3 Dec 1814	North Carolina	32	ditto
2647	James Campbell	*Volontaire*	7 Apr 1815	New York	36	ditto
2696	William Read	*Racehorse*	3 Jun 1815	Portsmouth	25	ditto
2733	Henry Burleigh	*Bennett*	2 Dec 1814	Newmarket	21	ditto
2740	David Chult	*Salvador*	3 Mar 1815	Salem	31	ditto
2848	Fred Hawley	*Royal William*	5 Feb 1815	Wilmington	23	ditto
2854	John Potter	Impressed	5 Oct 1814	Philadelphia	32	ditto
2942	Charles Baker	*Atalante*	30 Jan 1815	Virginia	19	ditto
2957	Josh Glodding	*Rattlesnake*	14 Mar 1815	Rhode Island	31	ditto
2990	Ed Powsland	*Frolic*	8 Jun 1815	Beverly	45	ditto
3035	Rich Studdy	America	3 Nov 1814	Virginia	30	ditto
3054	Henry Holding	*Sultan*	6 Mar 1815	Boston	27	ditto
3100	Jacob Eph Pinkham	*Monmouth*	25 Sep 1814	Mass.	22	ditto
3103	John Collins	ditto	8 Oct 1814	Philadelphia	24	ditto
3134	John Haywood	*Scipion*	6 Apr 1815	Maryland	25	ditto
3141	Wm. Williams	Impressed	27 Oct 1814	Georgetown	22	ditto
3187	Henry Sherriden	*Scipion*	24 Jan 1815	New York	22	ditto
3222	Peter Barry	*Jalouse*	26 Nov 1814	Salem	39	ditto
3271	William Meads	*Snapdragon*	24 July 1815	North Carolina	20	ditto
3297	J. Pettingall	*Enterprise*	7 Oct 1814	Salem	18	ditto
3376	Josh Windyer	*Growler*	6 Jan 1815	Marblehead	21	ditto
3434	Thomas Jones	ditto	23 Feb 1815	Baltimore	38	Cook
3442	J Williams	*Clorinde*	1 Feb 1815	Martha's Vineyard	26	Seaman
3459	John Bateman	*Chasseur*	23 Nov 1814	Baltimore	18	ditto
3470	Henry Thompson	*Prince*	21 Feb 1815	New York	28	ditto
3485	Dan Nash	ditto	14 Feb 1814	Dorset	31	ditto
3522	John Davenport	*Sabine*	10 Jun 1815	Easthaven	21	ditto
3544	Placid Lovely	*Hawk*	1 Nov 1814	New Orleans	29	ditto
3547	William Coleman	ditto	5 Nov 1814	North Carolina	21	ditto
3549	Lewis Brien	ditto	5 Nov 1814	North Carolina	24	ditto
3571	Sam Harrison	ditto	6 Jan 1815	North Carolina	21	ditto
3574	Wm Johnson	*William*	2 Nov 1814	Charlestown	25	ditto
3582	Henry Burbidge	*Greyhound*	25 Dec 1814	Washington	26	ditto
3588	Jacob Peterson	*John*	4 Nov 1814	Rhode Island	22	ditto

3595	Daniel Heny	*Frolic*	25 Jan 1815	Salem	22	Prize Master
3629	Lawrence Peterson	*Nonsuch*	8 Jan 1814	not given	?	Seaman
3656	John Thomas	*Elbert Gerry*	25 Oct 1814	not given	?	ditto

taken from ADM 103/ 90

3733	Nath Curren	*Lizard*	1 Jun 1815	Salem	22	Gunner
3756	John Kelley	*Alfred*	29 Mar 1815	Marblehead	62	Seaman
3795	John Raysden	*Pike*	14 Feb 1815	New York	32	ditto
3821	Peter Amos	*Invincible*	18 Feb 1815	Martha's Vineyard	22	Passenger
3827	Albert Mingo	*Quiz*	25 Oct 1814	New Orleans	29	Passenger
3842	Thomas Parker	*Dominique*	5 Nov 1814	Delaware	22	Seaman
3847	Uriel King	ditto	3 Feb 1815	Mass.	22	Seaman
3862	James Barnett	*Busy*	8 Dec 1814	Pennsylvania	56	Mate
3874	Lewis Stove	*Tickler*	21 Nov 1814	Conn.	22	Seaman
3879	Charles Monte	*Fame*	21 Feb 1815	San Antonio	22	ditto
3896	Abm Tomkins	*Governor Shelby*	3 Nov 1814	New York	36	ditto
3900	Peter Birch	*Prosperity*	13 Mar 1815	Philadelphia	57	ditto
3901	James Cateret	*Mary*	11 Nov 1814	Talbot	22	ditto
3936	John Washington	*Rolla*	6 April 1815	Savannah	25	ditto
3953	Tim Gardner	ditto	15 Jan 1815	Rhode Island	19	ditto
3981	William Gibson	*Rattlesnake*	22 Oct 1814	New York	22	ditto
3985	John Turney	ditto	5 Apr 1815	Mass.	23	ditto
4011	Josh Gladding	ditto	14 Mar 1815	New Jersey	37	Gunner
4030	Sam Lilley	ditto	16 May 1815	Boston	19	Seaman
4041	Francis Hobday	ditto	24 Feb 1815	Gloster	25	Marine
4069	David Read	*America*	14 Nov 1814	Wiscasset	21	Seaman
4194	Richard Smith	*General Kempt*	14 Apr 1815	Salem	24	ditto
4219	James Tucker	*Liberty*	28 Apr 1815	Long Island	24	ditto
4231	John Brissons	*Bunker Hill*	24 Jan 1815	Baltimore	32	ditto
4236	Charles Williams	*Pilot*	9 Mar 1815	New London	22	ditto
4326	John Carson	*Fiere Facias*	16 Oct 1814	New Orleans	26	ditto
4333	Richard Smides	*Flash*	6 Mar 1815	New York	17	ditto
4356	Sam Boardby	*Fiere Facias*	29 Mar 1815	Baltimore	29	ditto
4423	Isaac Harman	*Elbridge Gerry*	9 Nov 1814	Mass.	24	Q. Master
4460	Josh Long	*Fame*	29 May 1815	Mass.	21	Seaman
4479	David Simonds	*Enterprise*	22 Jan 1815	Mass.	18	ditto
4486	Joseph Lackey	ditto	4 Feb 1815	Marblehead	30	ditto
4549	Thomas Cooper	*Union*	8 Nov 1814	Mass.	34	2nd Mate
4556	Isaac Jones	*Hussar*	23 Jan 1815	Boston	22	Seaman
4628	William Brown	*Ulysses*	20 July 1815	New York	30	ditto
4705	James O. Cussar	*Volunteer*	7 Dec 1814	New York	39	ditto
4707	Stephen Jones	ditto	4 Nov 1814	New York	27	ditto
4718	James Jones	*Hussar*	27 May 1815	New York	27	ditto
4730	Joshua Fowler	*Theban*	30 Jan 1815	Boston	30	ditto
4737	Gideon Porter	*Acteon*	22 Mar 1815	Newport	32	ditto

4739	Jerry Gardner	a brig	1 Mar 1815	Rhode Island	27	ditto
4755	William Adam	*Africa*	15 Mar 1815	Colchester	22	ditto
4785	Thomas Greaves	*Port Mahon*	23 Feb 1815	Boston	28	ditto
4788	Jacob Sawyer	Impressed	25 Oct 1814	Providence	27	ditto
4798	William Knabbs	*President*	26 Feb 1815	Baltimore	22	ditto
4810	Pedro Joseph	ditto	25 Feb 1815	Guadaloupe	26	ditto
4811	N. Mendoza	ditto	25 Oct 1814	Carthegena	28	ditto
4820	St Yago Compichi	ditto	16 Jan 1815	Carthagena	18	ditto
4824	Amb Leman	ditto	24 Oct 1814	Carthagena	19	ditto
4825	Jose Almeno	ditto	3 Nov 1814	Carthagena	16	ditto
4826	Martin Aubury	ditto	17 Feb 1815	Carthagena	19	ditto
4836	John Johannes	ditto	8 Jan 1815	St Thomas	55	ditto
4846	John Jennings	*Hawk*	22 Feb 1815	Martha's Vineyard	18	ditto
4848	William Adams	ditto	24 Apr 1815	North Carolina	22	ditto
4850	Eben. Simonds	Gave himself up	12 Jan 1815	Newburyport	20	ditto
4851	James Adams	*Greyhound*	6 Nov 1814	North Carolina	20	ditto
4853	Edw. Evans	*North Star*	5 Jan 1815	Virginia	27	ditto
4856	Luke Rogers	*Fairy*	13 Nov 1814	North Carolina	24	ditto
4871	Jacob Morrell	*Fox*	27 Apr 1815	Mass.	22	ditto
4884	Wm. Loveridge	*Saratoga*	6 Apr 1815	New York	18	ditto
4886	Charles Fisher	ditto	6 Apr 1815	Delaware	33	ditto
4893	James Congdon	*Goree*	11 Nov 1814	Rhode Island	19	ditto
4917	John Menillo	*Rattlesnake*	18 Nov 1814	Baltimore	21	ditto
4930	Josh Gwynn	*Herald*	22 Feb 1815	Salem	18	ditto
4956	Asha Allan	ditto	14 Nov 1814	New Bedford	37	ditto
4958	Nicholas Smith	ditto	9 Jan 1815	Richmond	25	ditto
4967	John Baptiste Allen	ditto	21 Nov 1814	Africa	40	ditto
4995	Isaac Simondson	*Invincible*	20 Nov 1814	New York	20	ditto
5008	Anthony Lamb	*Grand Turk*	22 Nov 1814	Conn.	19	ditto
5014	D. Miller	*Mammouth*	23 Feb 1815	N. Jersey	26	ditto
5019	Sol Marshall	ditto	20 Nov 1814	Mass.	27	ditto
5025	M. Gennifon	*Syren*	12 Nov 1814	Baltimore	25	ditto
5052	John Polland	*Ida*	23 Nov 1814	Brazil	27	ditto
5053	Isacher Bray	ditto	20 Nov 1814	Cape Ann	23	ditto
5054	Josh Palmer	ditto	17 Nov 1814	Portsmouth	18	ditto
5063	Amos De Bates	ditto	18 Nov 1814	Hamburg Con.	22	ditto
5064	Joel Perigo	ditto	24 Nov 1814	Conn.	28	ditto
5074	Sylas Denham	ditto	14 Nov 1814	Boston	21	ditto
5089	John Adams	ditto	3 Dec 1814	Boston	27	Sailing Master
5095	Eman Jose	*David Porter*	25 Nov 1814	Portugal	20	Seaman
5105	David Taylor	ditto	19 Jun 1815	Philadelphia	19	ditto
5108	Josh Andrews	ditto	21 Nov 1814	Ipswich	21	ditto
5116	William Harris	*Portsmouth*	24 Nov 1814	Portsmouth	16	ditto
5118	Ramos Coffee	ditto	4 Dec 1814	New York	26	ditto
5137	Thomas Rowlinson	*Calabria*	26 Nov 1814	Virginia	22	ditto

5140	George West	Gave himself up	27 Jan 1815	Delaware	48	ditto
5144	Rich Holstein	*Baroness Longerville*	25 May 1815	Virginia	33	ditto
5232	James Roth	*Mary*	29 Dec 1814	Norwich	25	ditto
5240	James Davis	*Yorktown*	26 Feb 1815	Savannah	25	ditto
5245	Benj. Marshall	*Minden*	27 Mar 1815	Ilsborough?	23	ditto
5247	William Mista	*Atlantic*	13 Feb 1815	Virginia	36	ditto
5314	Tho. Thompson	*Thomas*	16 Jun 1815	Brooklin	32	ditto
5321	Thomas Jarvis	*Industry*	25 Jan 1815	Marblehead	18	ditto
5375	William Packer	*Derby*	28 Nov 1814	Barnstable	20	ditto
5376	David Turner	ditto	17 Mar 1815	Boston	23	ditto
5439	Wm Smart	*Elephant*	5 Dec 1814	Virginia	23	ditto
5500	Rueben Mitchell	No. 2 Gunboat	11 May 1815	Maryland	29	Gunner
5537	Richard Robert Lee	*Amelia*	20 Jan 1815	Mass.	23	Seaman
5553	Joseph Perkins	*Lacey*	20 Apr 1815	Mass.	18	Boy
5559	William Young	*Levant*	21 Jan 1815	Beverly	29	Seaman
5571	Thom. Simmonds	*Saratoga*	20 Jan 1815	New Bedford	55	ditto
5604	Sam Tophouse	Taken at Washington	11 Feb 1815	Washington	32	Soldier
5626	John Butler	*Semiramis*	23 Feb 1815	Pennsylvania	52	Seaman
5629	P. Queenwell	*Walker*	27 Jan 1815	Dartmouth	33	ditto
5647	Martin Sutton	*Lion*	22 Feb 1815	New Bedford	26	ditto
5656	Rob Adams	*Herald*	5 Feb 1815	?	?	ditto
5657	Ventus Conkland	ditto	23 Jun 1815	New York	20	ditto
5691	Jesse March	*Mcdonough*	5 Feb 1815	Mass.	29	ditto
5698	Dan Archer	*Grand Turk*	14 Jan 1815	Salem	22	Prize Master
5706	Arch Allen	*Harpy*	3 Mar 1815	Mass.	20	Seaman
5743	John Devinas	*Ohio*	12 Apr 1815	Salem	18	ditto
5744	Josh Dennings	ditto	12 Apr 1815	Mass.	26	ditto
5750	Stephen Stacey	ditto	16 Mar 1815	Marblehead	35	ditto
5788	George Brown	*Ocean*	11 Feb 1815	Pennsylvania	31	ditto
5793	Ebz. Holbrook	*Derby*	9 Mar 1815	Weymouth	24	ditto
5811	Sam Williams	*Scorpion*	15 Mar 1815	Mass.	31	ditto
5819	Moses Bailey	ditto	17 Feb 1815	Pennsylvania	21	ditto
5839	Phillip Blasdon	4 Reg Rifles	17 Jan 1815	New Hampshire	35	Soldier
5842	Shadrach Snell	1 Reg Rifles	16 Mar 1815	Rhode Island	19	Fifer
5847	Smith Sheldon	Militia	19 Jan 1815	Rhode Island	25	Soldier
5853	Elisha Holford	*Barfleur*	5 Jan 1815	New York	19	Seaman

taken from ADM 103/91

5883	Dan Bodge	*Harlequin*	16 Jan 1815	Arundel	23	ditto
5888	John Stone	ditto	5 Jan 1815	Arundel	44	ditto
5889	John Seapatch	ditto	7 Feb 1815	Mass.	12	Boy
5895	John Whittan	ditto	18 Jan 1815	Portsmouth	20	Seaman
5976	Silus Squibb	*Harpy*	18 Mar 1815	New London	21	ditto
6068	Geo Moore	*Chasseur*	29 Mar 1815	Boston	35	ditto
6112	Wm Fernald	*Harpy*	23 Jan 1815	Kihi ?	24	PrizeMaster

6126	Rich Lee	*Grand Turk*	19 Jun 1815	Marblehead	25	Seaman
6149	Josh Tremerin	*Mars*	4 Jun 1815	Philadelphia	19	ditto
6169	John Flowers	*Lion*	6 May 1815	Boston	56	ditto
6264	Wm. Robinson	*Plutarch*	18 Apr 1815	Philadelphia	40	ditto
6371	Joseph Haycock	*Syren*	20 Mar 1815	Portland	55	Gunner
6406	J.L. Osborne	*Portsmouth*	24 May 1815	Newburyport	18	Seaman
6442	Josh Salisbury	*Jemmett*	13 Mar 1815	Newport	22	Passenger
6451	Jacob Hentey	ditto	16 Apr 1815	Salem	17	Seaman
6504	Henry Campbell	Gave himself up	22 Mar 1815	Delaware	28	ditto
6514	John Jack	*Orontes*	14 Mar 1815	Baltimore	36	ditto
6515	John Peterson	ditto	1 Jun 1815	Albany	31	ditto
6520	Thomas Jackson	ditto	7 Apr 1815	New York	14	ditto

Researched by Principal Officer Ron Joy HMP Dartmoor, February 1989 in the General Entry Books of Dartmoor Prison (1813–15), further researched in October 1995.

Ron Joy found 267 in the General Entry Books ADM 103/87–91. The noted American historian Ira Dye found four more American deaths in other records, not in the General Entry Books, but the author has now included them in the above list. The missing names are:

2990	Ed Powsland	*Frolic*	8 Jun 1815	Beverly	45	Seaman
4011	Josh Gladding	*Rattlesnake*	14 Mar 1815	New Jersey	37	Gunner
5140	George West	Gave himself up	27 Jan 1815	Delaware	48	Seaman
5743	John Devinas	*General Putnam*	12 April 1815	Salem	18	ditto

This now makes a grand total of 271 American prisoners of war who died in the Dartmoor Depot between the years 1813 and 1815 during the War of 1812; many thanks to Ira Dye (USA) for checking my records from his superb database.

Appendix Five

PLAN OF DARTMOOR PRISON

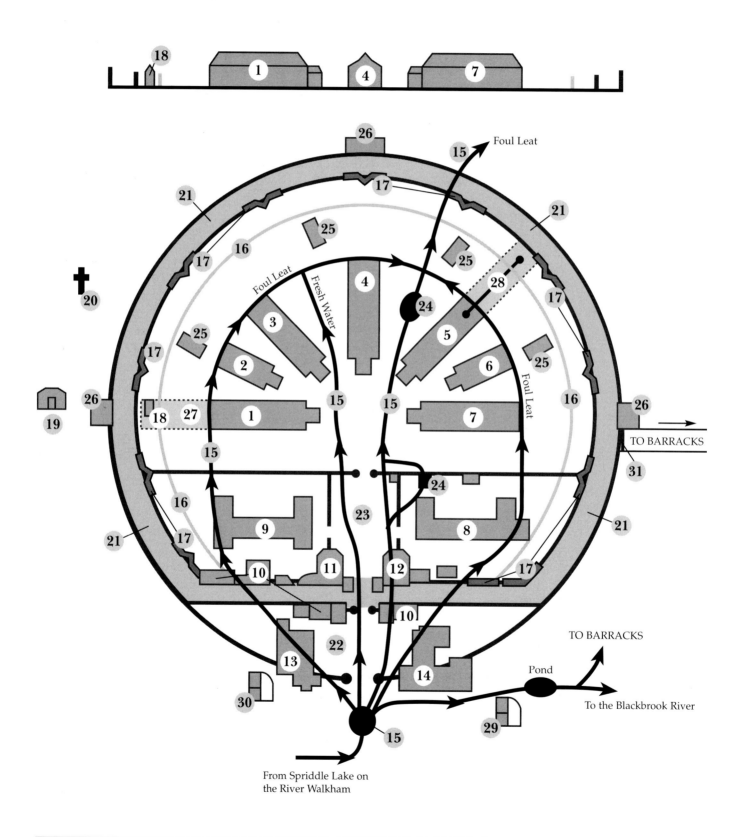

Foul Leat

Fresh Water

Foul Leat

Foul Leat

TO BARRACKS

TO BARRACKS

Pond

To the Blackbrook River

From Spriddle Lake on
the River Walkham

KEY TO THE PLAN OF PRISON
(all built 1806–12)

1	No. 1 war prison now F-wing
2	No. 2 war prison now demolished (now under all-weather sports field)
3	No. 3 war prison now demolished (now under gym)
4	No. 4 war prison now the Church of England chapel
5	No. 5 war prison now demolished (now under C-wing)
6	No. 6 war prison now old kitchen (roof has been lowered)
7	No. 7 war prison now demolished (now under A-wing)
8	Built as petty officers' prison, when the Americans arrived in 1813 it was used as additional barracks, now admin, classrooms, etc.
9	Built as the infirmary, many French and American prisoners of war died here
10	Staff houses, assistant surgeons, matron's quarters etc.
11	Gatekeeper's house, he lived here with his family
12	Provision store, this had a lookout box on the roof about 3-feet square, to enable a soldier to keep watch on the marketplace when prisoners were there, later tea boat, now governor's office
13	Surgeon's house (now works dept)
14	Agent's house, then convict governor's house, now prison officers' mess
15	Water tower with the leats feeding all the buildings
16	A paling fence, if any prisoner crossed this fence he would be shot from the embattlements
17	Embattlements, manned by soldiers at all times
18	Cachot (punishment block)
19	Dead house, used to store dead prisoners until a burial party took them out
20	Approximate area for burying prisoners, removed and reinterred in the French and American cemeteries on the orders of Capt. Stopford in convict times
21	Military road, soldiers were marched around here to the embattlements
22	Agent's Square, the agent was the Royal Naval captain in charge of the depot
23	Marketplace, prisoners were allowed to buy provisions here from market traders
24	Bathing places, one large one for the seven war prisons, a smaller one for the petty officers' prison
25	Drying sheds (inside the paling fence)
26	Guardrooms: north, east and south guardrooms
27	Modern G-wing is superimposed on the plan to show that it was built over the cachot (No. 18) (dotted line)
28	Shows the 1880 excavations 9 (dotted line) for the new convict hall. These excavations uncovered the escape tunnel dug by the American prisoners of war in 1813–14. This tunnel, according to the American prisoners got to about 40 feet from the boundary wall – shown here by a line which would be about that distance from the wall
29	Agent's coach-house and stables, the Agent's coachman lived here
30	Surgeon's coach-house and stables; the surgeon's coachman lived here also
31	Postern gate lintel inscribed by a French prisoner of war

Opposite: *Plan of the war prisons 1812 to 1816, showing fresh water supplies and the foul leats, which were conveyed to Sir Thomas Tyrwhitt's land at a place called Broken Barrow.*

Appendix Six

ILLINOIS SOCIETY
OF THE WAR OF 1812

In January 2001 the then governor, John Lawrence, asked me if I would help Burton L. Showers, Secretary-Treasurer of the American cemetery clean-up project at Dartmoor Prison.

As well as cleaning up the cemetery, the object was to provide a permanent memorial with all the names of the American prisoners of war who had died at the Dartmoor Depot during the War of 1812. A US Navy petty officer, Doug Harris, serving at RAF St Mawgan, Cornwall, was offering labour from the Navy boys serving at that base to do the physical part of the clean-up. Burton, who was to collect funds in America to pay for the memorial, asked me to supply the names of the American dead, and instigated the making of some cast-metal plaques with the names in raised lettering, by an American firm.

I provided the list of 271 names, as detailed in Appendix One. At this stage, another American officer, Captain Somerville, became involved, and it was arranged that in future the Americans would take responsibility for the maintenance of the American cemetery. It was also decided that instead of plaques, a stone with the names carved on it would be erected, paid for with the monies collected in America. This is the position as I write in May 2002. In due course the memorial will be placed in the refurbished cemetery, seating will be placed there, along with two flag poles, and possibly a small car park for visitors.

I hope that something similar will be done with the French cemetery next door, as well over 1200 Frenchmen lie buried there, as opposed to the 271 Americans. This project is a truly momentous one and all credit is due to those involved. My thanks to the former governor, John Lawrence, for instigating it, and of course to the present governor, Graham L. Johnson, for making it all possible, and for his welcome assistance and compassion in the project, which is much appreciated.

A general view of the prison and some quarters post-mutiny of 1932. The photograph was taken possibly in the late 1930s or early 1940s.

BIBLIOGRAPHY

Abell, Francis. *Prisoners of War in Britain, 1756–1815.*

Andrews, Charles. *The Prisoner's Memoirs, Dartmoor Prison*, printed 1815.

Atholl, Justin. *Prison on the Moor.*

Dartmoor Prison Works Department Archives, various plans and documents.

Dartmoor Prison Archives, Governor Gambier's letters 1853.

Dartmoor Prison Muniments Room Archives.

Dartmoor Prison Archive photographs, courtesy various departments/ author's collection.

Devon Record Office, Exeter. Diocesan Records (Chaplain's house 1813 accession 5720A/PB1-16) and Faculty Petitions 3-4-5-6-9 ref rebuilding of St Michael's Church, Princetown.

Dye, Ira. 'Essays in Maritime History', chapter in *Ships, Seafaring and Society*, edited by Timothy J. Runyan.

Ex-convict, An. *One who has endured it, five years' penal servitude 1878.*

Exeter University. *Reports of the Directors Convict Prisons*, courtesy Dr Fordyce.

Felknor, Bruce, and Kimberley Van Derveer. *Perez Drinkwater letters home*, Bruce Felknor@usmm.org, USA.

Grew, Major B.D. *Prison Governor.*

Marblehead Historical Society at the Jeremiah Mansion Marblehead, courtesy, Marion Gosling, USA.

Huntsberry, Thomas V. and Joanne M. *Dartmoor (War of 1812) Prison, USA.*

Novak, Rynell. *National Society US Daughters of 1812.* USA.

Plymouth and West Devon Record Office. Captain Hawkins papers (accession 380–450).

Thompson, Governor Basil. *Dartmoor Prison.*

Tullett, Tom. *Inside Dartmoor.*

Rhodes, A.J. *Dartmoor Prison 1806–1932.*

Webb, Major General Sir Joshua KCB 1793–1863. *Prison Service Journal*, April 1965 (IV No.15 page 26).

Western Morning News. 'Princetown: Its rise and progress', William Crossing, 1906.